Two of More
Original Works of an Unsung Storyteller
written by Brian Todd Barnette
Published by Bits and Peaces Productions, LLC.
copyright 2018 Brian Todd Barnette and Bits and Peaces Productions
"Coming Back to Leave" original copyright 2012
"Canonize Me" original copyright 2011

ISBN- 9780692195840

Library of Congress Control Number: 2018911581

"Canonize Me" short film adapted and directed by Miguel Miller, Miguel Miller Productions.

"Coming Back to Leave" originally appeared in script for the short film "No Time to Change My Mind" Adapted and Directed by Miguel Miller, Miguel Miller Productions, and written by Brian Todd Barnette copyright 2011

This is a work of fiction. Names, characters, business, events and incidents are the products of the author's imagination. Any resemblance to actual persons, living or dead, or actual events is purely coincidental.

TWO of MORE

Original Works of an Unsung Storyteller

Brian Todd Barnette

A Note From the Author

In early 2010, I had been having a personal, and existential crisis. I had recently relocated back to the town where I grew up. One of the things I was struggling with, besides health and finances, was how I hadn't followed a long held dream of being a writer and publishing something. Admittedly, I had only ever finished one particular project, but that was part of the problem. Why didn't I apply myself to this dream?

Some twenty-five years earlier, after a break up of a personal relationship, I sat down and wrote out my feelings in the form of a short fable. So I took these drawings and manuscript for the illustrated short story and was lucky enough to find a publisher in North Carolina that wanted to take a chance on it. My first book!

"Stone Upon Stone" was published in 2011. It got several great reviews, and I had seen a dream realized. The publisher later closed, and I re-released it myself and it is still in print, gratefully.

That led me to want to try other forms of writing in which I had always been interested. "Canonize Me" came about as I was searching social media groups for information on how to write screenplays. Thanks to Facebook I was able to find a group in Miami that was looking for someone to write a spec screenplay for a short movie they wanted to film.

The Director, who had produced several short films already, had the raw bones of an idea but wanted a full and complete story. So I wrote the screenplay for this story, called "Canonize Me." The Director liked it enough to adapt, and produce it, film it, and enter it into film festivals. The basis of the story is of a man who had died and thought he was worthy of sainthood. I developed this story into that of such a man who must take a brutally honest look at his life, and how his actions could be viewed by those actually affected by them. The short was amazingly accepted into the 2012 Cannes International Film Festival Court Métrage (short film) category. Wow! To me it was a watershed moment.

I had now realized more of a dream than I could have thought possible. And I wasn't finished. I wanted to do more. The Director challenged me to write a short script with one or two actors, and come in with a running time of about ten minutes. I wrote a short, then titled "No Time to Change My Mind" and the team again adapted it, filmed it, and also entered it into film festivals as well.

I was motivated to actually flesh out this short script into a full length story and thus wrote "Coming Back to Leave." The format may not be perfect when it comes to how scripts and screenplays are written, but as an exercise in creativity I am very proud of it. I have decided to have it published in this form, even as I am rewriting it as a novel and hope to complete that at some point as well.

The story itself takes place in a very recent timeline, sometime before the landmark United States v. Windsor, 570 U.S. 744 (2013) which effectively ended the discrimination against marriage equality for Gay and Lesbian couples. Yet, the misunderstandings and prejudices presented in this story still exist.

But the real story is how we live our lives, and how we think of the love and relationships we share. We spend so much time in memory. Whether we are recalling the good times or the difficult, we live and relive so many moments and they reinforce the emotions we have. Sometimes I wonder if love strengthens our memory or if memory builds and rebuilds the love we feel.

Although I have not been financially rewarded for the scripts it was exciting to know my name would be in credits in places like the Internet Movie Data Base, and that my name appeared in such renowned places as the Cannes International Film Festival.

My hope as an artist is that I will grow and develop my voice, and that I will create something meaningful that touches others.

Keep sharing stories.

Brian Todd Barnette

Also by Brian Todd Barnette
"Stone Upon Stone" ISBN 13: 978-0-692-78067-1

"Stone Upon Stone" is an illustrated short story about the challenges of communication in relationships.

One day I realized I had lived half my life, but my life had only been half lived.

Grateful to be awake now.

-Brian Todd Barnette

I am grateful to the CIEHAWK Media Team of the Center for Innovation and Entrepreneurship at the University of North Carolina at Wilmington.

They helped me realize a dream and recognize my own creativity.

Please support your creative friends.

Canonize Me

Screenplay
by
Brian Todd Barnette

Canonize Me

OPEN ON VARIOUS VISTAS OF SUN-LIT CLOUDS.

NARRATOR VO
There is an ancient story of the most beautiful prayer. A learned man was traveling into the city and he passed by a poor man. The poor man was muttering with his eyes closed and his head lowered in prayer. The learned man rides on. On another visit to the city, he passes the same poor man again and again hears him muttering in prayer but this time he makes out what the man is saying. The poor man is reciting the alphabet over and over. "You there," the learned man says to the poor man. "What is it you are doing?" The poor man replies, "oh, please forgive me. I am not an educated man and I do not know the prayers that you must know. I recite the alphabet and I ask that the Lord rearrange the letters into the words that He finds pleasing." At this the learned man scoffs and feels in his heart a feeling of disdain for the poor man. Immediately an Angel of the Lord appears and addresses the learned man. "From this day on, YOUR prayers will no longer be heard in Heaven, for it is this prayer, the prayer of the most sincere that we find pleasing and sings in the heart of the Lord your God." The learned man is left humbled. For it was the intention of the poor man to please the Lord that rang the bells of Heaven.

INCREASING LIGHT FROM OUT OF FRAME RESULTS IN TOTAL WASH OUT OF SCENE;

FADE TO BLACK

FADE IN

INTERIOR - ALL WHITE ROOM - POV OF MAN OPENING HIS EYES.

There are muffled voices and all we can see is darkness on the far side of room with silhouetted figures. There are three figures in the room, walking slowly back and forth and they are each backlit by a single color of light, one is red, one is blue and the other yellow.

                    HOLLY
    (to the others in the room) I think we have him.
              (to the man) George?

INTERIOR - DARK ROOM - NO PARTICULAR TIME

                                FADE TO BLACK

                                      FADE IN

SMALL DARK ROOM WITH NO DETAIL EXCEPT A TABLE AND A CHAIR ON ONE SIDE WHICH FACES THREE CHAIRS ON THE OTHER.

George Goodman sits on one side of the table. Beside him is a leather briefcase. He sits facing the three figures back-lit by the primary colors. Back-lit in red is what looks to be a tall woman with long hair but is very obviously male wearing woman's clothing, this is Holly. Next to Holly back-lit in yellow is a young woman, Martha, pretty but plain and holding what appears to be a baby wrapped in a blanket. Martha is rocking and patting the infant though we do not see or hear it. Seated next to Martha is a very shabbily dressed man, mid to late 50's in age, who has the appearance of a "homeless" person, slightly dirty, ragged clothes including a military jacket with the name "Emmanuel" on it. He is back-lit in blue light. This is Jésus.

                        HOLLY
    George, there is great love here for you. Are you
                     aware of that?

George looks slowly from one to the other.

                        GEORGE
                 What's this? Am I dead?

                        HOLLY
    Dead? That's not for us to say. You are no longer
    among the physical. But you are still in a state of
    what we call "separation." This is not part of your
     physical experience but you have yet to make a
                       transition.

George appears weary and lets out a sigh. The young woman, Martha, holding the infant does not look up and he has yet to meet her eyes. Jésus has a look of total calm and regards George with a soft and easy expression on his face.

                        HOLLY
      You still have a simple consciousness. Some
       things may take a moment to understand.

                        GEORGE
    Am I to be judged? I was a good man, I was
    practically a Saint in my life. Surely that must be
                        evident.

HOLLY
(smiling slightly) Judged? No. The idea of "Counselor" may be appropriate. We must decide what happens next. The next step. Next in time. That is up to you.

GEORGE
And who are you then? You seem familiar, as if I should know your names. What do I call you? What is the last thing I can recall?

HOLLY
What do you recall? Where were you before you were here?

GEORGE
I'm not certain. There seemed to be a large crowd and a lot of noise.

Behind George, a six-paned window appears and on it a scene.

CUT TO

EXTERIOR - CIVIC PARK SETTING - DAYTIME - SOUTHERN TOWN

George is giving a speech. The sound is muffled and unintelligible to us. He is at a podium on a lawn with a crowd standing around him, in the near background a municipal building. The crowd is a mix of people who periodically clap during the speech. Flanking George are men in suits and ties. Clean cut, wearing "campaign" style buttons. We understand that this is a rally or political "meet and greet" of some kind. There is the sound of gunfire and then screams.

Window scene goes black.

INTERIOR - SAME SMALL ROOM - CONTINUOUS

                    HOLLY
Is that the last thing you recall?

                    GEORGE
No. There is something else. I can smell disinfectant. I hear engines and traffic. Something smells burned as well. It feels crowded. Someone is yelling.

The scene in the window changes.

                                      CUT TO

INTERIOR - AMBULANCE - DAYTIME

POV of George looking up as several EMT's are working feverishly over him. The siren wails and the EMT's shout directions back and forth. We can see a bloody shirt being cut off and pulled to the side and just below POV we can tell George is wearing an oxygen mask. One of the EMT's is putting an IV in George's arm. The window scene fades out.

                                        CUT TO

INTERIOR - SAME SMALL ROOM - CONTINUOUS

George looks at Jésus.

                    GEORGE
(to Jésus) Do you not talk?

Holly and Jésus exchange a look. Martha does not look up but continues to gently rock and pat the infant.

GEORGE
And what about her? (motioning to Martha) Does anyone else talk to me here?

HOLLY
Now isn't the time for frustration or for being angry. They have actually tried many times to talk with you. Let us do what it is we need to so that a decision can be made. You will be given all the information you need. Call me Holly, I can counsel you. Jésus will guide you as well. Martha cannot look directly upon you and speaks to you through us.

GEORGE
(in a quiet voice) Why does that make sense? Where have I been told that before.

HOLLY
You made the statement that you lived the "life of a saint." What do you mean by that?

GEORGE
If I am no longer in physical form, it must be that I am no longer "living." I think I was shot. I don't think I survived it. I thought that after we die, we are judged for our lives. I am certain I was an honorable and just man. I feel as if I am to be judged then I need to say that I know I was a good man.

JÉSUS
Can you explain?

George is surprised by the sudden involvement of Jésus and turns to address him directly.

GEORGE
Well, foremost, I treated everyone I met with compassion and respect. I was awarded for it on many occasions in my life. Humanitarian awards, special recognition for working with non-profits, donations to my church and to the community...

HOLLY
Ah, yes. The George Goodman legacy. You raised money for several organizations and helped champion the scholarship for a school. The "George Goodman" Academic Achievement Scholarship for your Alma Mater. I believe you insisted on naming it after yourself and also being able to have first right of refusal on any new products created by the participants when developing their senior projects. Did you not end up making more money by having an authorship rider on the patents created over the years?

George is at a momentary loss.

HOLLY
More money than all the endowments you made in sum total?

GEORGE
It takes money to make money. That program created several civic leaders and leaders of industry for the city. It created jobs and kept people working.

HOLLY
I am sure you can justify it. But lets talk more about the manner in which you treated others. Do you recall what you would tell friends and co-workers about those who pan handled or begged in the streets?

GEORGE
Well, I supported soup kitchens as well. And homeless shelters.

George has a flash of recognition. He looks at Jésus with wide eyes.

GEORGE
You! I remember you! You stood outside of the homeless shelter and wouldn't come in. This was years ago. You refused to go inside to get anything to eat or seek shelter. It was cold that year.

Another scene plays in the window of Jésus outside of a big brick building.

CUT TO

EXTERIOR - DIRTY CITY STREET - DAYTIME - DATE UNDETERMINED

Jésus is having an exchange with a man in a suit that we only see from the back. Jésus is obviously bundled up against the cold. He is smiling but shaking his head nervously. He reaches out to take the hand of the man in the suit who recoils and pulls away.
'

The window scene fades out.

CUT TO

INTERIOR - SAME SMALL ROOM - CONTINUOUS

GEORGE
I remember you asked me to just go inside and bring out something for you to eat. I recall that it made me feel a bit angry. There was help for you just inside. All you had to do was walk in!

JÉSUS
Do you recall what you did? What you thought? What did you tell others about that exchange?

George hangs his head a bit sheepishly, as if the memory now fills him with a bit of guilt.

GEORGE
Well, what I remember is feeling indignant. As if all that we did was still somehow not enough for you. I didn't understand why you wouldn't just go inside. Some part of me wanted to drag you inside. I feel shame now, but I was mad at you. I told my colleagues that some people were beyond helping. I know that isn't so. It was my pride saying that.

JÉSUS
Do you recall what you said to me under your breath?

GEORGE
(voice cracking) I said "so starve."

JÉSUS
There is an old proverb. "True charity sees the need, not the cause." The man you met that day, the man I seem to you, was a war vet. He was suffering from a post-traumatic stress. He found it almost impossible to go into strange buildings. He had seen several of his fellow troops ambushed once and they were all killed. He himself barely survived. He had been left for dead. Upon his return to civilian life, he was never able to accept the help that had been offered him. He only found help at a local church that had to close after a fire. He lost his only refuge. And the way you now recall dealing with him, was a chance for you to welcome him. And inasmuch as the way you treated him, you treated the Divine.

Jésus pauses.

George cannot look at him. He looks down at his own hands folded on the table. Although there is much that Jésus is saying, his tone is always loving and kind. He never raises his voice. His voice is filled with compassion.

JÉSUS
Do you understand the idea of seeing the Divine in others? That the way you treat others is an opportunity to interact with the Divine. And rather than take the opportunity to bestow kindness and understanding, you treated me from your pride and with indignity. You wanted someone to pat you on the back for helping build the shelter, yet one personal act of kindness was lost.

At this point, Martha begins to hum softly as she rocks and pats the infant. Wish a sweet voice she sings what sounds to George like a made up song.

MARTHA
(singing to the infant, without looking at anyone else in the room) I love you, you're perfect. I love you, that's everything. You are part of me, I am in your heart, you are in my heart. You are loved.

George looks on with a puzzled expression. He turns to Holly.

GEORGE
And why do I know you? Did I have an encounter with you?

HOLLY
Do you remember any reason why you and I would have crossed paths?

GEORGE
No offense, but I don't know any lessons I could have learned from…well…anyone like you in my life. I don't have anything against….people like you. To each their own, I say. I know I never did anything to put you down.

HOLLY
In your life, do you remember someone who worked in one of the companies from whom you sought campaign support when you were running for city councilman? There was someone you met, someone who headed the public arts council?

GEORGE
I think so. You always wore a neck scarf right Always a neck scarf with a butterfly motif? I do remember now. I remember you catching me staring at you and I told you that the scarf reminded me of a picture I had seen in a magazine. I tried to make you feel...to feel...OK.

HOLLY
The person you knew me as was trying to make a difference in the community. I wanted to create a public art space. To encourage kids and young people to find their self expression through art. Do you remember that? Do you remember what you told the Mayor about the kind of people who worked with the public?

GEORGE
Vaguely. I think I had told the Mayor that even though I had nothing against you, the public may base their perceptions on his projects on how you....looked...and that may leave a negative image in their minds. But I wasn't the ONLY one who thought that! You must admit, most people would have felt uncomfortable not knowing how to relate to you! Should they think of you as a man? As a woman?

HOLLY
In the world beyond yours, there are no such things as either men or women. There is neither free man nor slave. We are all one. We are all spirit. We appear to you this way now because we are part of what you accepted. You spent your life as a Catholic, but you didn't even fully experience that path to God.

                          GEORGE
              How was I not a good Catholic?

                           HOLLY
It's not about being a good Catholic. I am speaking
about your experience of God. There are as many
paths to God as there are individuals, but you
never even fully experienced the one to which you
say you were attached. You say you lived the life
of a "Saint" and yet you never even looked to a
Saint for guidance, for comfort. You didn't pray
the prayers, you stopped taking communion, you
had not made the sign of the cross in years.
Whenever you were inside the most beautiful
church in the state, your mind was a hundred
miles away, in a small corner office, thinking of
                      anything else.

A new window scene comes into focus. It's a small
office.

                                            CUT TO

INTERIOR - NONDESCRIPT OFFICE - DAYTIME

We see "Holly" sitting at a desk, looking at a small
hand mirror, adjusting the scarf around her neck.
As she looks up she sees a man standing in front
of her. We see him only from the back. The smile
fades from Holly's face and is replaced with a
solemn, almost "hurt" look and she lowers her
head.

                                            CUT TO

INTERIOR - SAME SMALL ROOM - CONTINUOUS

George looks down at his hands again. He seems to be lost in thought. Martha begins to say the "Glory Be" prayer

MARTHA
(to no one) Glory be to the Father...

George looks at Martha as she recites this prayer to the infant, which we have still yet to see or hear.

A new image appears on the window behind George.

CUT TO

INTERIOR - UNDETERMINED LOCATION - UNDETERMINED TIME/DATE

A simple image of a pair of hands holding the rosary. The hands are not discernible as either male or female.

MARTHA (VO)
...Glory be to the Father,

THE SCENE IN THE WINDOW FADES OUT

CUT TO

INTERIOR - SAME SMALL ROOM - CONTINUOUS

MARTHA
...world without end....world without end....world without end

Martha goes silent again.

            JÉSUS
(quietly, not looking at anyone) And so it is.

            GEORGE
I am beginning to feel like my life is being reduced down to a few instances where I just didn't do it right. But I feel like that's an unfair assessment. I really did try my best. (sighs heavily)

George regards Holly silently. Holly smiles at George again with a look of deep compassion. Her eyes are soft on him. George looks over to Jésus without expression. Jésus offers the same smile as Holly and brings his hands together as if in prayer and bows his head to George. George looks at Martha. She has yet to look up at him or engage him directly in any way. She hums softly but has a small sweet smile on her face as well.

            GEORGE
And what of her? When did I meet her in my life? What circumstance where I gave a sincere effort yet, was there a time I failed to completely honor her?

            JÉSUS
You need not be defensive. This is for your benefit. For you to understand fully what happens next. There really is great love here for you.

            GEORGE
No. I do NOT feel it. I feel condemnation. I feel as if I just do not measure up. How does anyone measure up. What are we cut out for? Who can be perfect?

JÉSUS
Who indeed? Whats perfect is the process. In any moment you strive to be even incrementally closer to Truth. That is perfect. That is all we must do.

GEORGE
And her? (indicating Martha) I am searching my memory. But she has not looked upon me. How do I....how DID I know her?

HOLLY
What do you feel happens next? What is after your experience of life? Where are you going?

GEORGE
What? I get to choose? Do you mean Heaven or Hell? I would choose Heaven! What is it? Where is it?

HOLLY
Your "life" experience is the only one in which you have a separate sense of self. An identity of self outside of the All. Heaven, as you know it, is just a concept for the physical realm. To be part of the "ALL" is beyond your comprehension, It is a level of wholeness for which you do not have words or any point of reference. All you knew of as YOU will be no longer. Your mistakes, your hurts, as well as any feelings of separation. As waves are not separate from other waves but all circumstances that created them may be different, they all return to the ocean. Without want or need, you can return to Source. Hell is another concept for the physical realm, and in truth, it is a feeling of total separation from the

All. Its a feeling of disconnection so total that you will never feel whole.

GEORGE
But sameness is hated in our lives. To be individual is the goal. It is rewarded. How can perfection turn that idea on its head?

HOLLY
But you do not have the capacity to understand how it really is. In your world, pure white light is made of the reflection of all spectrums of light. There are really endless levels within the pure white light. In your world, the absorption of all light actually becomes the deepest black. Perfection is the reflection of pure light. Inclusion, light and perfection. Separation is the absorption. Darkness, separation and lack of any characteristics. Simple but you may understand the opposites of a spectrum.

George seems lost in thought again. His brow is furrowed and he seems borderline exhausted.

Martha begins to sing again. This time it's a song from the 1970's that had been refashioned into a soda commercial. As she finishes the first chorus, George, in a flash of recognition, looks again at her, wide-eyed.

GEORGE
Martha? YOU! I remember you! You helped me produce my first speech while we were in college You were amazing. So beautiful and so dedicated. I think we even dated! (to the others) Is that her? Is that the same young woman?

JÉSUS
You have part of it correct. She fell in love with your drive, your ambition and the electric atmosphere you created wherever you went. She believed in your vision. She felt at her young age that she could actually make something of her life. She had come from a family where the mother was long suffering and the father was silently aggressive. Abusive with indifference. She was on the edge of becoming alive. Do you remember what happened between you two?

George's face begins to crumble. He becomes overwrought with emotion. He doesn't cry but his words are almost strangled in emotion.

GEORGE
We went out after a debate. We had too much wine and made love. I woke up thinking that she would become a burden. She looked at me with such admiration and expectation.

HOLLY
What did you say to her?

A new scene appears behind George in the window.

CUT TO

INTERIOR - SMALL ART STUDIO - DAY - UNDEFINED DATE

Martha sitting at a canvas. The canvas is actually blank. A door close behind her.

CLOSE UP

Martha's face, and her eyes close and smile fades.

Window scene fades.

CUT TO

INTERIOR - SAME SMALL ROOM- CONTINUOUS

GEORGE
I told her that we could not be a couple. She wanted too much. She needed me too much. I needed more excitement than she generated. I told her she needed to learn more about the world.

HOLLY
It may be hard to hear it this way, but she wasn't able to keep the baby.

GEORGE
(choking) The baby?

HOLLY
She conceived that night. She had a very difficult pregnancy. You don't recall that she dropped out of school because you were riding a wave of acceptance and support that would carry you to many successes in your life. How could you know what happened to one young woman? You knew her only briefly.

GEORGE
(still emotional) What happened t the baby?

HOLLY

She was almost to term. She miscarried. Her family had turned their back on her and she felt guilty that she was not able to even become a mother. She had thought having a baby would bring into her life all the love she felt she wanted to give. And she lost her only son. In her grief, her life took a turn for the worse. She escaped into drugs, selling herself and eventually into an unfulfilled life living on the fringe. Most people just didn't believe in her. In her goodness. In how much love she really could offer. The rest of the details aren't important.

GEORGE

Then what can I do? What are my choices? What happens now? You say somehow I will know or I will choose Heaven? My understanding of it is that I get to forget all of my mistakes? Hell means I get to remember them compounded? I don't want to be separate, I want things to be right.

HOLLY

(indicating the briefcase that has been beside George the entire time.) In your memory are all the things that can be done differently. All the times you thought you were right but you were still coming from a profound sense of YOURSELF only. Not selfish, but not concerned for anyone other than yourself either. You can choose to rejoin Source. Say good bye to all that was and experience paradise in Source, or you can...

GEORGE

(interrupting) Can I do it over? Can I do it again? Can I take the chance that I DO know better? I CAN bring others closer to truth. Can I do it again?

He gets more emotional and impassioned

Holly and Jésus share a solemn glance and then look at Martha as she continues to rock the baby.

HOLLY
You can choose so. You must choose freely. It happens when you decide. To rejoin Source is a final choice as well. All the effort will be over.

GEORGE
Then I choose to do it again! I can make it work. life is full of opportunities to make it right. To bring us all to the Truth. For all of us to reflect the light. Life would not have been created if it wasn't possible. Too many of us agree that its worth it.

MARTHA
(indirectly) The choice must be free will.

GEORGE
(grabbing the briefcase) Then I choose it. I choose it all over again.

Light comes from the window scene and grows brightly until the whole scene has been engulfed in the light. It recedes a bit and we see Holly, Martha and Jésus stand.

Martha drops the blanket open and we see it is now empty. Jésus and Holly come to stand on each side of Martha. Jésus has a tear in his eye.

> HOLLY
> The choice is always the same.

> MARTHA
> They go back and live separately. (pause) They always choose "Hell."

A new scene appears in the window. We see a newborn being held in a doctors hands.

INTERIOR - HOSPITAL DELIVERY ROOM - UNDEFINED DATE

We see a baby crying, covered in birth matter, being cleaned by a nurse. From off camera we hear the doctor then the mother over the cries of the infant.

> DOCTOR
> You have a healthy baby boy.

> MOTHER
> Thank God.

FADE TO BLACK

END

Coming Back To Leave
Love and Memory

An Original Screenplay
by
Brian Todd Barnette

Coming Back to Leave
Love and Memory

BLACK

FADE IN

EXTERIOR - SMALL BUNGALOW: MORNING: PRESENT DAY

telephone ringing
RING RING

INTERIOR - SAME HOUSE - KITCHEN -CONTINUOUS

FADE IN

Varying shots of what seems to be an empty home as telephone rings; a living room, a bedroom.

RING RING

Shift focus to notice man in mid 30's drinking coffee at wooden table in a modest kitchen. He gets up and crosses room to the phone on small telephone-table, he stops and looks at it while it continues to ring. Then it stops. He pauses then returns to kitchen table and sits back down, toying with a pen as he stares at a blank note pad on the table.

PANNING OUT

He looks around and we see more of the kitchen. It is clean, with traditional cabinets and just a few appliances and knick-knacks on the counter. The man sets down the pen, and we hear his thoughts, in a vague, almost matter-of-fact tone. Not cold, but no real hint at depth of any emotions.

                    MAN(VO)
I can't believe what I'm doing. I am going to actually leave you. It's like I am the last one to really get it. After such a long time of trying my best, I can't fix this.

He stands up and begins to wander around the house as we continue to hear his thoughts.

INTERIOR - SAME HOME- LIVING ROOM - CONTINUOUS.

Man walks into living room from kitchen.

                    MAN(VO)
It's strange. To think we lasted as long as we have. Even our friends said we were mismatched early on.

He touches several objects in the living area as he reflects; a small framed poster of a stage show with a pair of theater tickets, two sea-shells, a small in print of a cat's paw.

> MAN (VO)
> You were the one who wanted to get married someday. You always said you would convince me. I thought I may reconsider, but I know I will never get married. I am convinced it wouldn't last. Especially now.

He walks into a short hallway.

INTERIOR - SAME HOME - BEDROOM - CONTINUOUS

Man walks into bedroom from hallway.

CUT TO

INTERIOR - SAME HOME- BEDROOM- CONTINUOUS

He walks through bedroom to closet and opens closet door. He pulls a suitcase from a shelf, takes it back into the room and opens it on the bed.

CUT TO

INTERIOR -SAME HOME- CLOSET - CONTINUOUS.

He returns to the closet. It is neatly arranged with all men's clothing. He slowly begins choosing various articles of clothing. His hands move slowly over the clothes stopping occasionally on some articles; a pair of jeans, a novelty T-shirt, several colorful ties from a tie hanger.

                    MAN (VO)
So different...and yet we wore each others clothes. What's mine? What's yours? Does it matter? Are these your T-shirts and jeans? Are these my short sleeved shirts and khakis? Does that matter? I could buy a whole new wardrobe and still look the same on the outside. It's the inside that has changed ...broken. I can't dress that up.

                                        CUT TO

INTERIOR - SAME HOME- BEDROOM - CONTINUOUS

Man returns to the bed with items of clothing; jeans, pants, shirts, etc. He begins to fold several articles of clothing into the suitcase. he goes to a bureau and chooses socks, under garments from the drawers and a wrist watch from the top of the bureau. He fingers a few other items of jewelry on the top of the bureau.

                    MAN (VO)
Things I always thought but never asked... which one of us had the sunnier disposition? Who makes better jokes? Now it's different questions. Which friends will

treat me the same? Who really likes "me" and not just "us?" Do I even care?

> RING RING

The phone rings again and he stops and listens but still does not move to answer it.

> RING RING

Telephone rings a few more times then stops. He finishes packing the suitcase with the clothes and wanders into the bathroom.

> CUT TO

INTERIOR - SAME HOME- SMALL BATHROOM CONTINUOUS.

There are two different toothbrushes, two different types of razors.

> MAN (VO)

Were the odds against us anyway? You believed in God and went to church, I never could. You believed in a lot more than I did. What does your faith say about what I am doing? Would it have helped if I had prayed?

He grabs a bottle of cologne, a razor and then picks one of the tooth brushes. He looks at both of them for a moment. He takes them both.

                    MAN (VO)
Do you still love me? Do I still love you? I'm sure I do, but I have to block that out or I couldn't do this. And I have to.

Man returns to bedroom.

                                                    CUT TO

INTERIOR - SAME HOME- BEDROOM- CONTINUOUS

He has brought the items from the bathroom and puts them into the side of the suitcase.

                    MAN (VO)
I know it's not your fault. I know its not "MY" fault. Hell, it's not anyone's fault. Still, I wonder if I could just be angry. Or hate you.

Man walks out of bedroom carrying suitcase.

                                                    CUT TO

INTERIOR - SAME HOME - LIVING ROOM - CONTINUOUS

He brings the suitcase into the living area sets it down. He walks toward to the kitchen, he passes a small table and he looks down at a grouping of pictures in various frames. Our vantage point is from behind the frames as he looks down, slowing as he passes.

CUT TO

INTERIOR - SAME HOME - KITCHEN- CONTINUOUS

Entering the kitchen he glances at the silent phone. He then moves to the table and picks up the coffee cup from which he had been drinking, washes it in the sink, dries it and sets it onto a small shelf with only one other coffee cup on it. The two cups are different in color and design.

>MAN (VO)
>No, it wouldn't be easier to hate you.

CLOSE UP

Man is adjusting the two coffee cups, moving them closer together with handles facing the same direction.

NORMAL SHOT

>MAN (VO)
>I'd never be able to do this unless I loved you.
>Completely.

Now his cell phone rings as we see it on the small table in the kitchen. He picks it up and looks at the caller ID. We see the name "Patti." He answers it. We only hear his portion of the conversation as he moves back into the living area.

                    MAN
 Hey Patti-O. (Pause) Yes, I am about to leave. (pause)
         No, it isn't easy... this is what he wanted.

Man exits kitchen back to living room.

                                        CUT TO

INTERIOR - SAME HOUSE - LIVING ROOM- CONTINUOUS

He moves to a box that is on a table and pulls out an urn. We see that it is a simple funerary urn that would hold ashes of cremains, and a label on the box reads "Martin Raymond; Gilbert Funeral Home."

                    MAN
Yeah, it was nice. That's what you say right? That's what everyone says. "It was nice." (Pause) More for them than for me. (Pause) He wanted to be taken to the beach. I owe that to him. (voice cracks) I'm leaving him there.

MAN (VO)
No, I couldn't leave you unless I loved you. I'd want you with me always. Even like this.

He sets the urn down and turns away.

CAMERA VIEW BEGINS TO WIDEN OUT SLOWLY.

Man returns to phone conversation as scene begins to fade.

WHITE OUT.

MAN
I will call you when I land. I can finish things here any time. (Pause) I just can't believe I'm doing this.

Muted conversation continues as scene becomes completely white.

FADE TO WHITE

FADE IN

INTERIOR - SAME HOME - KITCHEN MORNING - TWO WEEKS EARLIER

From view looking out of kitchen window, we see the same man. Todd Gordon, mid 30's, dark brown hair, dressed in a semi-professional manner, drinking coffee over the sink. Light jazz is playing from a small MP3 player and he sips his coffee casually.

Another man, Martin Raymond, mid 30's, lighter features, comes in from exterior room which is the living room. He is dressed in cut off sweat pants and a novelty T-shirt. He has obviously just awoken. He comes shuffling up behind Todd, wraps an arm around his waist and nuzzles the back of his neck. He breathes in deeply.

                    MARTIN
          Mmmmm.... I love your cologne.

                    TODD
          Don't you mean "essential oil?"

Todd smiles and leans back against Martin, laying his free hand over Martin's.

                    MARTIN
          Still. Smells good. What's in it again?

                    TODD
          You made it up for me. All I know is it smells like us.

                    MARTIN
          Oh yeah, thats right. It's "us" I smell. Good to know.

Martin yawns and stretches in a large sweeping extension of his arms then wraps them both around Todd, kissing the back of his neck once. He lets go and (continued) looks around, rubbing his hands through his hair. He walks over to the sink.

MARTIN
Anyway, Good morning. Are you running off early?

TODD
Yeah, I didn't want to wake you too early. The flight isn't until 10 but its a Friday. Ugh. Late February up north. Not looking forward to it. I'd better check for delays again.

MARTIN
Make sure you packed your toothbrush. YOUR toothbrush. Don't just take both of them again.

TODD
Jeez....

Martin reaches onto a small shelf by the window and takes down a mug. Its different than the one Todd is using, mismatched. He walks over to the stove and takes an old pyrex coffee pot and pours himself a cup. He adds too much sugar and a little bit of cream. Todd watches, bemused.

TODD
Hummingbird.

MARTIN
Neanderthal.

TODD
Love you.

MARTIN
Love me too.

Martin pulls out one of the two chairs at a small cafe table in the center of the kitchen and sits down. His long legs splayed out. Todd brushes one of his legs against one of Martin's. Martin pushes back slightly, in a gesture of endearment.

TODD
What are you doing today? No class?

MARTIN
I'm...

MARTIN AND TODD
...nothing but class.

TODD
Ba dum bump.

MARTIN
I am going in to finish some grant requests for the spring. Not too much to do, but I don't want to put it off.

Todd leans over and they clink their coffee cups together before he finishes his in one last gulp. There is a coffee ring left on the table. Martin lifts his cup to reveal another intersecting it. He traces them with his finger.

Martin
(quietly) With this ring...

Todd returns to the sink to wash it out and dries it with a small dish towel. He places it back on the shelf from where Martin had taken his cup.

MARTIN
Do you want me to go with you to the airport? See you off with a big sloppy kiss and a wave?

TODD
Not again.

Todd leans in again and kisses the top of Martin's head.

TODD
How about you meet me in Chicago on Saturday afternoon? We can make it a getaway. I have plenty of miles. Could be fun. We could do the music thing, maybe Abby is performing, hang out with Vince.

MARTIN
(visibly excited) Really? Want to?

TODD
Why the heck not? Why else do I work so hard?

MARTIN
(playfully, as if accepting a challenge) I will you know. I will get on that plane and meet you there!

TODD
Do it mister! I dare you!

MARTIN
Double dare?

TODD
Double DOG dare.

MARTIN
Seriously? Do you want to?

TODD
You just love to have me beg you for things don't you?

MARTIN
Well.......

TODD
(in a kids voice) pppllllleeeease!

The two men laugh. Todd groans.

                    MARTIN
Ok, SURE! I'll do it! Just DON'T tell my boyfriend. He's going to be in Chicago at a boring lecture. He's the jealous type, he'd kill you.

Todd laughs again.

                    MARTIN
It'll be fun! I'm in. I'm SO in. Really really?

                    TODD
Argh. REALLY really.

                    MARTIN
We can fly back together. We haven't been on the same plane in ages! Fun, fun, fun. I expect an all-star weekend, just saying.

                    TODD
So now I am in competition with your boyfriend?

Both men laugh again.

                    MARTIN
This has put me in a music mood. I feel like singing some retro 80's.Standards. No new stuff. Old school.

Maybe even some country. Tanya Tucker, Lacy J Dalton... or Jessi Colter!

Martin gets up to pour himself another cup of coffee, he walks to a small phone table where there are two cell phones and a house phone. Picking up one of the cell phones, he checks the time. It is 8:05.

MARTIN
uh-oh. You'd better whippity scoot! I'm excited! After I do a little bit of work at the school, I will come home, finish laundry and pack. I can take the first flight available tomorrow. Do you want me to book the ticket? I can check into who is playing any of the clubs and give Vince a call too.

TODD
No, I'll book a ticket when I get to the airport, so I can use bonus miles. I am going to have an hour or so to kill. Although you may have to confirm this afternoon. My flight gets into Chicago just after noon local and the event is just for a few hours tonight. I can leave after the morning conference and meet you about 2 pm. Just check your email for flight info and confirmation later. Cool?

MARTIN
Cool daddy-o. I'm excited, we haven't done anything on spur of the moment in a while!

TODD
By the seat of our pants?

MARTIN
On a whim.

TODD
We be spontaneous and shit.

MARTIN
...and shit.

TODD
Ok, you... go shower and then get to school! I will call you from the airport before take off if I have any problems booking a flight. Bring a scarf this time. Its still winter you know.

Todd kneels down in front of Martin and Martin musses his hair gently. They lean in and kiss, not deeply, but they do linger.

MARTIN
Love you.

TODD
Love me too.

Todd stands up and smiles down at Martin who closes his eyes and smiles a big, silly, grin. Todd heads out of the kitchen into the living room.

                    MARTIN
     (singing) I'm not Lisa... my name is Julie...

INTERIOR - SAME HOME- LIVING ROOM
CONTINUOUS.

Todd picks up a messenger bag, exerts a bit getting it over his shoulder. He walks by a small playbill of a Broadway play which has two tickets framed with it. He picks it up, kisses the tips of his fingers and then places them on the glass in the frame. He sets it back down then and then extends the handle on a small suitcase by the table, pulling it with him.

                    TODD
          (calling out) Ciao bello!

                    MARTIN
     (from the other room) GO! (then sweetly) I miss
                you already! GO!

Todd opens the door and drags the suitcase out with him, pulling door closed behind him.

                                        CUT TO

EXTERIOR - SAME HOUSE- CONTINUOUS

Todd pulls the suitcase down a small walkway to his car, opens the back door putting the bags inside, then gets into the front seat. He pauses, looks for a moment at the house before starting the car, backing out and pulling away.

> CUT TO

INTERIOR - SAME HOME- LIVING ROOM- CONTINUOUS.

Martin comes into the living room from the kitchen in time to see Todd pull away. As he heads back into the kitchen he notices the framed playbill, straightens it, smiles.

INTERIOR - SAME HOME - KITCHEN - CONTINUOUS.

Martin goes to the sink, washes out the coffee cup, drying it with the small towel and places it beside Todd's. He arranges them side by side with the handles facing the same direction. Mismatched but a pair. He has a small smile on his face and begins to sing in a mock country style, but with a nice voice.

MARTIN
(singing) Mama, I've always loved cowboys, Mama, I
                never will change...

Martin walks out of the kitchen and into the living room.

INTERIOR - SAME HOME - BEDROOM - CONTINUOUS.

Martin enters bedroom from hallway, stripping off his T-shirt as he enters, he pulls a hamper from the corner, adds the shirt to the bundle inside, pulling out the liner and then pulls the drawstring on it, setting it beside the hamper. Then he disappears into the bathroom, all the while singing in a mock country style, getting a little louder over the sound of the water in the shower.

                    MARTIN
(still singing) ... why do I fall, for those crazy, blue eyes...

                                          CUT TO

INTERIOR - TODDS CAR ON BUSY HIGHWAY - CONTINUOUS

Todd is speaking through blue-tooth phone connection in his car. He is speaking with his office assistant Micky.

                    TODD
And then, do me a favor and try and extend into personal reservations at a hotel on the lake, maybe one that matches miles. Triple A. Try the W.

                    MICKY
            Senior citizen discount?
                                        CUT TO

INTERIOR - SMALL OFFICE - CONTINUOUS

Micky, Todd's assistant, is at a small desk. There are some calendars with dates circled and the word "CHICAGO" written in red. Micky is late 20's, kind of a hipster. Not feminine, but has a playful sense and can camp it with Todd in a casual manner. Micky goes to computer and Googles "Chicago Hotels".

                    MICKY
Do you want to trade in some S&H Green Stamps too?

BACK AND FORTH BETWEEN THE OFFICE AND TODD'S CAR.

INTERIOR - TODDS CAR - CONTINUOUS

                    TODD
Don't be rude. And find out if there is a hotel florist. I want a few small bouquets of daisy.

Silence for a moment.

TODD
Micky? You there?

MICKY
(deadpan) Gay.

TODD
AND your boss.

MICKY
(false enthusiasm) I mean 'how sweet!' Seriously, is this, like, some kind of anniversary or is it the Tony awards or something?

TODD
Nope. It's just what adults do in loving relationships.

MICKY
I guess it's nicer than a T-shirt for the morning walk of shame.

TODD
Voice of experience?

MICKY
Hey, YOUR man is the one with the nutty T-shirt collection.

TODD
(laughing) OK, yeah, you got me there. But no shame in his game.

MICKY
OK, buzz me when you're at the airport, I will let you know confirmations. I have to go now, we're having our "Todd's out of the office" party and it's my turn to sit naked in your chair.

TODD
Note to self, buy Lysol.

MICKY
(imitating woman's voice) Judy Bernley, please hold, Judy Bernley, please hold. This is Judy.

TODD
Now who's gay?

MICKY
click.

The call is disconnected, and Todd laughs. He sets the phone down and replays a bit of the morning in his mind.

               FLASH BACK

INTERIOR - TODD AND MARTINS HOME - EARLIER

Martin has just come up behind Todd, wrapping his arms around him.

> MARTIN
> Mmmmm.... I love your cologne.

> TODD
> Don't you mean "essential oil?"

Todd smiles and leans back against Martin, laying his free hand over Martin's.

> MARTIN
> Still. Smells good. What's in it again?

> TODD
> You made it up for me. All I know is it smells like us.

> MARTIN
> Oh yeah, thats right. It's "us" I smell. Good to know.

FLASHBACK ENDS

INTERIOR - TODDS CAR - CONTINUOUS

Todd smiles and laughs a bit to himself. He continues with a memory.

FLASH BACK

INTERIOR - TODD'S CAR - FLORIDA HIGHWAY - NINE YEARS AGO - DAYTIME

Todd is driving on a small road in Florida, they are pulling out of a nice neighborhood onto a two lane road, surrounded by lakes and small houses, some orange groves now and then. Martin is holding a small brown bottle in his hand, he takes the lid off and smells it. He closes his eyes.

> MARTIN
> Mmmm. This stuff is great!

> TODD
> Wow, your friend Patti was pretty cool. She must have been a hippie back in the day.

> MARTIN
> Yeah, she and I are "travelers on a star" together.

> TODD
> I'm glad I finally met her.

> MARTIN
> She rocks. (puts the brown bottle into a back pack) I totally dig this essential oil stuff. Im going to make some for us when we get back.

> TODD
> Like with patchouli? Nah, I've already got cologne.

MARTIN
But this stuff is awesome! And its organic, no chemically stuff. And it will help you think about me.

TODD
(Looks over and catches Todd's eye and winks.) How so?

MARTIN
You heard her. "Olfactory cuing" or something like that, enhanced "sense memory." Engages the whole body. I believe it. I mean c'mon, perfumes are a couple billion dollar a year industry. Must mean something.

TODD
Yeah, maybe. But if it doesn't smell good, or if it smells too "flowery," I am not wearing it.

Martin is looking out the window as they are passing some old orange groves. The trees are in bloom. He reaches over and turns off the air conditioning.

TODD
What? Are you nuts? It must be 90 degrees outside.

MARTIN
Wait...

Martin rolls the window down and takes a deep breath. The air is heavy with the fragrant orange blossoms.

>MARTIN
Pull over.

>TODD
What? No way. Why?

>MARTIN
Pppplleeeease? (mockingly)

>TODD
HA!

Reluctantly, Todd checks the rear view mirror and pulls over to the shoulder of the small highway.

>MARTIN
Roll down your window.

Todd rolls down his window.

>MARTIN
Now breathe.

Todd rolls his eyes slightly, but takes a deep breath. A small smile appears on his face.

CUT TO

WIDE SHOT

EXTERIOR - TODD'S CAR - FLORIDA HIGHWAY - CONTINOUS

View of Todd's car on side of the road, parked by orange grove.

CUT TO

INTERIOR - TODD'S CAR - CONTIUOUS

TODD
(quietly) Hey. Yeah... that is nice.

He opens his eyes.

MARTIN
No, no... keep 'em closed. Just breathe it in for a moment. Just.... breathe.

Martin and Todd sit quietly for a moment, both breathing in the heady scent of the grove of orange trees in blossom.

MARTIN
(quietly) Who knows when we will smell something like this again, but when we do, just know one thing....

TODD
What's that?

MARTIN
That I love you Todd. Really, really.

Todd opens his eyes, he sees Martin who has a silly grin on his face. Todd "chucks" him on the chin.

TODD
Oh wow.

MARTIN
Breathe that in. I love you. You don't have to say anything. But someday, if you smell this again. You WILL remember.

Martin reaches over, punches Todd playfully in the shoulder.

MARTIN
Yup. I'm definitely making us some homemade smell-goods.

Todd starts the car and they drive back onto the road, they don't roll the windows up and Martin continues to take deep breaths.

INTERIOR - TODDS CAR - CONTINUOUS

TODD
(singing "Would You Lay With Me") Would you lay with me, in a field of stone...

FLASHBACK ENDS

EXTERIOR - TODD AND MARTINS HOUSE - CONTINOUS.

CUT TO

INTERIOR - SAME HOME - LIVING ROOM - CONTINUOUS.

Martin is dressed in khakis, a different novelty T-shirt with a chambray shirt over top, he is carrying a worn leather messenger bag and a helmet for riding a motorcycle or similar. He pulls on an older, worn, motorcycle jacket, wrapping an orange scarf around his neck in a simple knot, tucking the ends into the jacket. He is still singing as he walks out of the front door, locking it behind him.

MARTIN
(singing 'Would You Lay With Me') Would you lay with me, in a field of stone...

EXTERIOR - TODD AND MARTINS HOUSE - CONTINOUS

Martin walks to the covered carport and unlocks a Vespa scooter, securing his messenger bag to the carrier. He puts on the helmet, pulling a big pair of sport sunglasses from a pocket of his messenger bag, putting them on. He starts the scooter and pulls out onto the residential street.

                                                                                                 CUT TO

EXTERIOR - AIRPORT - SAME DAY -

                                                                                                  CUT TO

INTERIOR - AIRPORT PARKING GARAGE CONTINUOUS

Todd exits his car, pulling his bags out. He presses button on key fob to lock car with a beep. He stops and double checks the pocket of his bag, pulls out the flight confirmation and has a relieved look on his face. He starts walking towards a sign that says "to all gates."

                                                                                                  CUT TO

INTERIOR - AIRPORT - CONTINUOUS

Todd enters airport terminal from sliding glass doors. The terminal is moderately busy with all the usual crowd, noises, etc. He heads off towards a check-in counter, pulling his small suitcase behind him. He steps into a line of about 10 other people and waits, as they are each assisted.

                                                                                                  CUT TO

INTERIOR - AIRPORT - CHECK IN - CONTINUOUS

Todd steps up to the counter, and he is greeted by Airline Ticketing Agent.

> MARYANN (TICKETING AGENT)
> Hello sir. How may I assist you?

> TODD
> (reading her name-tag) Hello MaryAnn, checking in, but also want to change a leg tomorrow, departing Sunday evening from O'Hare back to RDU Sunday rather than Saturday evening and purchase a ticket for my partner for a flight tomorrow, RDU to Chicago. I want to use some bonus miles. Here...

Todd pulls out a wallet and some papers, hands her two cards, one being an ID and the other a Frequent Flyer card.

> TODD
> RDU to ORD, O'Hare. 1 passenger, any flights before noon? Returning on same flight as me on Sunday?

> MARYANN
> Let's get you checked in and taken care of, and I'd be happy to book that. You are headed to Chicago, O'Hare, Flight 1307, departing Gate 17, arriving Chicago 12:10

p.m. local time. Flight is on time. I see you have flown with us quite a bit, and we thank you.

                    TODD
                 I thank YOU.

                   MARYANN
               Checking any bags?

                    TODD
No, I know how to pack like a pro. Just the one and a computer bag.

Todd places his carry-on onto the scale beside the ticketing desk.

                   MARYANN
             Wow, right on the money.

                    TODD
             This ain't my first rodeo.

                   MARYANN
(laughing) I guess not! You should give classes! You know, you are due for a special day. I'm going to put you into Row B if you'd like, a slight upgrade. You're only in the air for an hour and fifty minutes, but at least you can stretch your legs a bit.

TODD
You just made a great day even better. Don't spoil me too much or I may invite YOU to Chicago.

MARYANN
I'd love to but the Mrs. wouldn't like it. (winking at Todd) Too much to do this weekend.

TODD
(slightly surprised) Well, you go Maryann. Love to the Mrs. from me!

MARYANN
I will certainly tell her. For your trip to and from Chicago all flights direct, non-stop.

TOOD
It doesn't get any better. That's perfect. We can put him on same return flight?

MARYANN
It looks open, so I am sure that won't be a problem at all. Just to let you know, there is a slight travel advisory for Chicago later today, but you should be in before then. Freezing temps, high winds. Naturally.

Maryann types a moment or two in the system.

MARYANN
OK, you are set, here is your confirmed boarding pass, now let's check Raleigh to Chicago, tomorrow morning. Is a 10:20 flight workable?

TODD
Perfect. He's an early riser too. (winking at Maryann) That's practically lunchtime.

MARYANN
Great! I just need a name for now, unless you have all of the personal identification information on you?

TODD
Oh, yes.

Todd pulls his phone out and brings up information.

TODD
Just don't let on that it isn't all memorized. Well, except for birthday. And color preferences, ... inseam, jacket measurements, favorite movie, you know, the essentials.

MARYANN
As it should be. Let me read off his Drivers License number here, will he be able to confirm today?

                    TODD
Not a problem. I will text him after we book and let him
    know to take care of that. How crowded is that flight?
  Let me book that first class too. I need to burn up some
        of the miles and I may as well spoil HIM.

                  MARYANN
  Sounds like we are both pretty lucky. He is all set, I will
      print up the information for you and I can email
      confirmation to him as well, if you like.

                    TODD
              Right on. Here ya go!

Todd writes down Martin's email on the confirmation
and Maryann types it into the system.

                  MARYANN
  Done and done. You can begin boarding soon yourself,
  so have a great flight to Chicago and a great weekend!

                    TODD
  Maryann, you are a blessing. Thanks for your help.
    Make sure your lady knows you helped make my
                  weekend special!

                  MARYANN
          Oh, she KNOWS how lucky she is.

Todd smiles, taps the counter twice, walks away with his

bags. Maryann looks along after him. One of her coworkers, Carrie comes up behind her. Maryann rolls her eyes without Carrie seeing, and forces a smile.

CARRIE (COWORKER)
Maryann, he was a looker! I saw you guys smiling a lot and laughing. Flirt! Why are you so picky about the ones that ask you out?

MARYANN
Not on the market, Carrie. I've told you. Very happy, thank you.

CARRIE
Well, anytime you are ready to go to church with me, I have lots of respectable men who may help you see things in a normal way.

MARYANN
(A bit annoyed) No, but thank you, Carrie. Busy now. (to the next passenger) Yes, ma'am, I can help you...

The next woman in line steps up to Maryann's counter.

CUT TO

INTERIOR - AIRPORT - TERMINAL - CONTINUOUS

Todd is walking along, expertly dodging other travelers. He pulls his phone from his pocket dialing his assistant again.

MICKY
Todd Gordon's office, how may... oh. You again.

TODD
Any luck on the hotel? Flowers?

MICKY
What? That was like two minutes ago!

TODD
You may want to take a few moments and update your resume as well. Just saying.

MICKY
You have the best professional assistant on the block. And one who knows your darkest secrets. Just saying.

TODD
Remind me of that in your exit interview. Kisses. Seriously. What do we have?

MICKY
You're gonna want to be nicer to me. As it turns out, BOSS I have a friend, who has a cousin who works at the W Lakeshore and for regular rate you are actually being upgraded; perks to include a complimentary bottle of

champagne and lake view. I told them you were someone important. Oops, tiny white lie. I will now accept your gratitude.

TODD

Mea culpa. Flowers?

MICKY

Can you not do anything on your own? Fine. I will have flowers put on your card. And sushi.

TODD

I don't want sushi waiting for me. Three hours old. That's gross.

MICKY

Sushi is for me. All of this work makes it hard to find the time to eat a proper three squares a day.

TODD

Hey, sushi instead of a bonus. I win.

MICKY

Oh, its going to be a LOT of sushi then. There is a florist who can deliver, but I think they actually laughed when I asked for daisies. Maybe they thought I was in kindergarten. I wasn't really listening. But relax. I take care of everything.

TODD
You deserve ALL the nice things I don't ever say about you.

MICKY
Anything else needed for your life to be easier? Please say yes.

TODD
You know what? Why don't you finish normal stuff and take off early this afternoon. And sure, have some sushi on me.

MICKY
I will certainly let you pay for it. And thanks boss! I promise not to spoil myself... unnecessarily.

TODD
But before you leave, just verify the events tonight and tomorrow morning in Chicago. Email me if there are any changes. Have a good weekend.

MICKY
You got it. Tell Martin I'm the best.

TODD
click.

Todd presses the phone off, he steps into a long line to go through airport security. He starts to prepare by unlacing his shoes. As he approaches the TSA agent, he opens his laptop and powers it on as well as shows his phone. Placing shoes and bags onto scanner belt, he empties his pockets into tray. The TSA agent is pleasant in her instructions.

                    TSA AGENT
    (thick NC accent) Step up honey. Now turn around.

The scanner beeps only slightly on Todd's belt buckle.

                    TSA AGENT
    You're good baby, have a nice flight. Next please.

She had barely given Todd a look as he stepped to the end of the conveyor, taking his shoes, pocket items and bags. He slips his shoes on, tying them and heads off to the gate. He pops into a Starbucks and grabs a chilled bottle of a coffee drink. An attractive young woman gets behind him as he pays and attempts a flirtation.

                   YOUNG WOMAN (1)
                  A morning pick-me-up?

                        TODD
    Ha. Not really. I could use this as a creamer for my
      regular coffee. But I've had two cups already this
    morning. This is mainly because I have a sweet tooth.

The young woman laughs with him as he pays and leaves.

                              CUT TO

EXTERIOR - SAME TOWN - ROAD - 20 MINUTES LATER

The day is bright, but brisk. As Martin stops at a traffic light, he blows into his cupped hands, rubbing them together.

                    MARTIN
              Gloves. Gloves. Gloves.

The light changes to green and he continues. We see a sign that says "University traffic" with an arrow directing to the right. Martin turns right. Martin is maneuvering the scooter through light traffic, pulling into a small southern university campus. There are only a few pedestrians out on the grounds. Some jogging, some carrying back packs and the like. Two of the people on campus walking together wave as Marin drives by, beeping the horn on the scooter. He pulls up to a brick building into a space marked "faculty and staff parking," takes off glasses and helmet and pulls his messenger bag over his shoulder. He heads into the building.

INTERIOR - FACULTY BUILDING - HALLWAY
CONTINUOUS

Martin passes a group of three male students, maybe mid 20's at the oldest, they are talking amongst themselves.

                TROY (FIRST STUDENT)
It sucks. They didn't offer the class this semester. I either have to wait til fall or screw up my summer.

              SCOTT (SECOND STUDENT)
        So what. Take the summer class.

              BRAD (THIRD STUDENT)
Screw that man, who needs that one class?

              TROY (FIRST STUDENT)
         I do, idiot. It's required.

              BRAD (THIRD STUDENT)
           Plan better, bro.

              SCOTT (SECOND STUDENT)
        (to his companions) Hey look,

He motions to Martin as he passes by, who remains practically oblivious to them.

              SCOTT (SECOND STUDENT)
Isn't that that guy they interviewed last year about gay pride on campus?

BRAD (THIRD STUDENT)
Gay pride? What the hell, man.

SCOTT (SECOND STUDENT)
Yah man, they were after marriage equality and wanted to get the school to make a statement.

TROY (FIRST STUDENT)
So what? Why do you care?

BRAD (THIRD STUDENT)
(mocking) Yah, you interested? (laughs)

SCOTT (SECOND STUDENT)
Screw you.

BRAD (THIRD STUDENT)
Not in me, in (feminine voice) him.

SCOTT (SECOND STUDENT)
You're an ass.

TROY (FIRST STUDENT)
Screw both of you.

SCOTT (SECOND STUDENT)
That shit ain't funny. I didn't want to come to some school that supports a bunch of freaks.

Scott forces a laugh. They continue on their way. Martin has been oblivious to any of this. Martin enters into a room marked "Liberal Arts Faculty" by swiping a key-card. The door closes behind him.

INTERIOR - UNIVERSITY - FACULTY ROOM
CONTINOUS

Martin enters into a smaller cubicle that has his nameplate on the partition. He pulls out a chair, sets his bag on the desk, which is full, although neatly arranged, with stacks of papers, folders, a framed picture of Todd. He pulls a folder from a stack, his laptop from his messenger bag, opens it and turns it on. He is still singing classic country songs.

MARTIN
(singing 'Crazy') Crazy... I'm crazy for feeling so...
(pauses for a moment) lonely.

Martin pulls out a cell phone and dials a number. Waits a moment and then leaves a message.

MARTIN
Hey, miss Patti. Whats shaking? Todd and I are going to be in Chicago for the weekend. Score! We are going to try and see Vince, but give me a call. Still planning on being in Orlando with you for Easter. Peace out.

Martin presses button to end call. He lets out a big sigh and opens a folder.

CUT TO

INTERIOR - AIRPORT - CONTINUOUS

Todd is sitting in the terminal before boarding, sipping his drink and just looking around. He sees mostly single passengers, a few couples.

TODD
(to himself) No kids. (looks upward as if praying) Thank God.

Then he makes a face as if mocking himself. Todd types a text into his phone to Martin. "the pearl is in the river." He hits send. Smiles to himself, then thinks a moment, types another text, "in case you didn't get the movie reference, you're a go, flight is set, check email TTYL" He hits send. A moment later another text, "love me too" he hits send.

There is an announcement

VOICE ON P.A.
Attention passengers on flight 1307 non-stop Raleigh Durham to Chicago, we invite our premiere travelers to begin boarding. Flight 1307 Raleigh Durham to Chicago now boarding premiere passengers with proper

boarding pass. Please have your ID and boarding pass ready and available as you board. We welcome you and will begin boarding remaining travelers momentarily.

Todd gathers his bag and heads towards the gate attendant. He has his ID and boarding pass in one hand and his coffee in the other.

AIRPORT GATE AGENT
Hello sir, good morning. (checks Todd's information) Thank you sir, have a nice flight.

TODD
Thank you as well.

Todd walks down the gantry onto the plane, two flight attendants and a co-pilot are standing in the entry.

CO-PILOT
We won't have any of it on this leg, but this afternoon looks like it could get messy. I'm off the next few days and I don't want to spend it in Chicago.

SECND FLIGHT ATTENDANT
(to Todd) Hello sir, thank you (checking his boarding pass) You are seated right here (indicating a nice seat in the first row by the window)

> FIRST FLIGHT ATTENDANT
> May we get you a beverage before take off?

> TODD
> No, thank you.

Todd stashes his bag in the overhead and sits down as the Flight Attendants assist boarding of other first class passengers, which are only a few. He overhears one of the pilots still talking to the Flight Attendants.

> CO-PILOT
> What do you mean, you've never been marooned in Chicago? Or Minneapolis? That weather is brutal on schedules.

> SECOND FLIGHT ATTENDANT
> (girlishly) I guess I've just been lucky. But if you think we'll miss it, I guess we'll have to try our luck again.

> CO-PILOT
> Oh I see. (laughing) Don't tease an overworked man.

> FIRST FLIGHT ATTENDANT
> (Annoyed, whispers to Second Flight Attendant and quietly, yet Todd overhears) OK, good weather, bad weather, keep it in your pants.

The first Flight Attendant walks to the rear of the first class cabin as other travelers squeeze by, filling up the rest of the aircraft. Second Flight Attendant assists other passengers in first class.

Todd motions to the second Flight Attendant

> TODD
>
> Excuse me, has there been a weather update? Anything for tomorrow?

> SECOND FLIGHT ATTENDANT
>
> Just normal sleet and snow. And wind. Maybe a few delays but nothing too serious. It's not expected to last very long. Are you on another flight tomorrow?

> TODD
>
> No, expecting my partner to join me. Around noon.

> SECOND FLIGHT ATTENDANT
>
> I will double check and let you know shortly.

                      CUT TO

INTERIOR - UNIVERSITY - FACULTY ROOM
CONTINUOUS

Martin is typing on his computer. He gets up as a printer begins to print out a few documents. He pulls two large envelopes from a box by the printer, returns to his desk with these items. He begins to write addresses on the envelopes, then separates the papers into two piles, signing them on a few differing lines and puts them into the envelopes. His cell phone rings. Checking the caller ID, he sees that it is Todd sending a message that reads "Last text before take off. Call later. smooch." Martin smiles and straightens the items on his desk. He sets the envelopes into a folder with hand written title "for review" on it. He packs up his personal items, just before leaving his cubicle, he kisses the tip of his finger and presses it to the glass in the framed picture of Todd. He pulls the messenger bag over his shoulder, grabs his helmet and walks out of his cubicle, then out of the office, pulling the door behind him.

                                                                                                         CUT TO

EXTERIOR - UNIVERSITY PARKING - CONTINUOUS

Martin is seen coming from the Liberal Arts building, walking to his scooter. He adjusts his items on the scooters rack, puts on his helmet but doesn't secure the chin strap, starts his scooter and then pulls out of the parking area.

Martin heads out onto the highway, a bit busier now, he keeps to the right of the busy traffic. Up ahead we see that there is some road construction with cones, heavy machinery and some workers. It is causing a slight bottleneck of traffic. Martin waits in the traffic, still slightly off to the right. He keeps looking around to remain safe in the traffic.

                                                  CUT TO

EXTERIOR - SMALL HIGHWAY - SAME TOWN CONTINUOUS

                                                  CUT TO

INTERIOR - SCOTT'S (STUDENT) CAR

Scott and Troy are in Scott's car. Scott is in the driver's seat. They are the two students who passed by Martin a bit earlier on campus. From out of the front windshield, we see Martin on his scooter slightly ahead of them.

                      SCOTT (SECOND STUDENT)
      Look, there's your boyfriend on his girly-mobile.

                        TROY (FIRST STUDENT)
   Dude, give it a rest. Sounds like you're the one who's
                            interested.

                    SCOTT (SECOND STUDENT)
Screw you, I think they ought to kick his ass off campus. Figures he's a freaking liberal arts geek. I bet he's in the
                            theater too.

                TROY (FIRST STUDENT)
              Yeah, you've got it bad man.

                SCOTT (SECOND STUDENT)
              I'm gonna run his ass off the road.

                                              CUT TO

EXTERIOR - SAME HIGHWAY- CONTINUOUS

INTERIOR - SCOTT'S (STUDENT) CAR- CONTINUOUS

As they approach , they notice that Martin is staying off to the right side of traffic.

                                              CUT TO

EXTERIOR - SAME HIGHWAY - CONTINUOUS

Martin is starting to get a little hesitant on his scooter, cautiously looking around. As the traffic narrows approaching the road crew, there is less room for him and he will need to pull into the traffic.

INTERIOR - SCOTT'S (STUDENT) CAR
CONTINUOUS

                SCOTT (SECOND STUDENT)
              Watch this man.

Scott gets a look on his face of determination. He edges closer to the right side of the road approaching behind Martin on his scooter.

>TROY (FIRST STUDENT)
>What the hell are you doing man. You can't hit him.
>DUDE!

>SCOTT (SECOND STUDENT)
>(under his breath) Faggot.

Scott pulls directly beside Martin honking his horn and revving the engine of his car, causing it to lurch to cut Martin off. Martin struggles to keep right side up on his scooter, pulls off to the side of the road just, as a road-crew vehicle is backing up into the area. The road-crew truck is carrying a lot of equipment and veers to avoid Martin, also blowing the horn.

Martin struggles with the scooter, knocks his head on some of the equipment that extends beyond the side rails of the work truck. This causes his helmet to fall off and as he pulls back into the oncoming traffic, an approaching truck behind Scott's car is unable to avoid hitting the back of Martin's scooter and he is thrown off and into the street, where he is struck by another car in the adjacent lane. His body rolls a bit then comes to a stop.

INTERIOR - SCOTT'S (STUDENT) CAR - CONTINUOUS

Troy has watched the entire scene play out in the rear view mirror and he turns around in the seat.

                TROY (FIRST STUDENT)
     Holy shit! Dude! Holy shit! What did you do?

              SCOTT (SECOND STUDENT)
             (excited) Shit! (laughs)

Scott continues to drive away as the cars behind him come to a stop due to the accident. Scott speeds away.

              SCOTT (SECOND STUDENT)
    Shit, shit, shit. (then laughing) Can you believe that shit? Man, he got nailed!

                TROY (FIRST STUDENT)
Are you freaking kidding me? What the hell did you do?! You have to go back. That freaking car hit him, man!

              SCOTT (SECOND STUDENT)
HELL NO! He's fine. Nobody was going that fast. Don't be such a pussy! That shit was funny as shit!

               iTROY (FIRST STUDENT)
You're effing crazy! No way man! Dude, you gotta go back, he may be hurt!

SCOTT (SECOND STUDENT)
No way, I'm not going back there. Serves his gay ass right, driving a freaking fruit-scooter!

Scott notices the frantic look on Troy's face and starts to laugh again.

SCOTT (SECOND STUDENT)
Dude, chill OUT. That was nothing. Maybe he got a little banged up. A boo-boo. Seriously. We weren't even doing ten miles an hour! Relax, Nurse Nightingale. Sheesh.

TROY (FIRST STUDENT)
You are messed up. Seriously. Like, cold-hearted messed up. That was not even funny. What if he ain't OK?

SCOTT (SECOND STUDENT)
Then you can send him flowers and give him a sponge bath. Pussy! Grow up. He's just some queer teacher, big hairy deal. Damn, you're like a high school girl! Stupid damn faggots.

Troy goes silent, still with a frantic look on his face, as Scott continues to laugh, then turns up the music on the radio.

SCOTT (SECOND STUDENT)
I hope his little gay putt-putt is out of commission. Funny. HA! Funny as shit!

Troy just stares at Scott as they continue to drive away, taking the turn off of the highway.

                                             CUT TO

EXTERIOR - SAME HIGHWAY- CONTINUOUS

Scott's car turns off the road to the right and continues on its way.

                                             CUT TO

EXTERIOR - SAME HIGHWAY - CONTINUOUS

Back at the accident, Martin is still laying in the road, not moving. There is a small amount of blood in his ear, some obvious abrasions on his face. The driver of the car that struck him is on his cell phone, as he tries to direct the traffic away. Some of the road crew are bending over Martin, a few on their cell phones, some even taking pictures or video of the scene. The driver of the road-crew vehicle is explaining to his fellow crew...

                    ROAD CREW DRIVER
   I didn't hit him. It was that other dude, but it wasn't
   nobody's fault. He just pulled in and out of the lane! I
                    swear, I didn't hit him!

                    OTHER DRIVE TRUCK
He clipped my front bumper. I didn't hit him, he hit me.
Then that other dude (indicating the driver of the car)
                    hit him! Out of the blue!

                    OTHER DRIVER CAR
(on cell phone) please, hurry! He just pulled back into
the traffic, I couldn't stop! He's just laying in the street,
    I can't tell if he's awake! I was hardly going fast!

                    ROAD CREW DRIVER
... and then he just lost it! Pulled back into traffic! It just
                    happened like THAT!

The other driver, the one that struck Martin,
approaches the road crew. A police cruiser is pulling up
from the shoulder from the traffic, lights and siren on.
We hear another siren in the back ground.

                    OTHER DRIVER
Did anyone see what happened? I tried to miss him! He
                just pulled in front of me!

                                            CUT TO

INTERIOR - CHICAGO CAB - SAME DAY -A LITTLE
LATER

The taxi is driving toward town with the airport in the
background. Todd is getting himself situated in the car.

He pulls out his phone and sees the power bars indicating almost no battery life. He makes a frustrated, comical face. Dials a number, it starts to ring then phone goes dead.

                    TODD
              DAMMIT! Arrgh!

Todd looks through his computer bag, getting a slight bit frantic. He is searching for the power cord to his phone.

                    TODD
              Dammit, dammit, dammit....

                                              CUT TO

EXTERIOR - CHICAGO HIGHWAY INTO THE CITY
CONTINUOUS

The taxi gets into heavier traffic coming into the city. The skyline is evident.

                                              CUT TO

INTERIOR - HOSPITAL ER

Various scenes of Martin being rushed into the hospital, ER staff shouting directions and instructions, EMT carrying Martin's messenger bag and giving details to ER nurse. Normal hurry of a hospital ER.

CUT TO

EXTERIOR - CHICAGO HOTEL

Todd is getting out of the taxi, paying the driver and a curbside attendant is assisting with his bag. Todd nods a thank you as they enter the hotel lobby.

CUT TO

INTERIOR - CHICAGO HOTEL

Busy, with upscale clientele, mostly adults, dressed in business and professional attire. Todd heads to the check-in desk, a Front Desk professional smiles and they begin the registration process.

CUT TO

INTERIOR - HOSPITAL ER -

Doctors and nurses are checking Martin and adjusting IV's and monitors as he is wheeled again into another room.

CUT TO

INTERIOR - CHICAGO HOTEL - ROOM

Todd is entering from the hallway, dragging his bag with him. He sets everything down onto his bed and begins rummaging through, still searching for his phone charger. He cannot find it.

> TODD
> Peter Rabbit. CRAP!

Todd looks at the instructions on the room phone, dials the front desk.

> TODD
> (to Hotel operator) Yes, can you tell me the closest place to buy a phone charger? I know there is an Apple store on Michigan, but kinda hope there is something closer for now. (pause) Oh, OK. Thanks then.

Todd hangs up and then sits down on the bed. Thinks a moment. Picks up room phone again, dials a number. Waits as t rings.

CUT TO

INTERIOR - HOSPITAL ER -

Martin's phone is sitting amongst some of his belongings in a hospital room, silently ringing, with caller ID says "unknown" but the phone desktop shows a picture of Todd smiling. It goes to "MISSED CALL"

                                                          CUT TO

INTERIOR - CHICAGO HOTEL - ROOM

Todd leaves a voice message.

                          TODD
 Hey mister. Checked into the room, phone is dead and I
  forgot to pack my charger evidently. Leave a message
   for me, W, Lakeshore, room 525. Oh, its Todd calling.

Todd hangs up the phone, lays back onto the bed,
stretching. He is still for a moment, thinking back on the
morning.

                                                        FLASHBACK

INTERIOR - TODD AND MARTINS HOME - EARLIER IN
THE MORNING

We again see Martin, just awakened, coming up behind
Todd and wrapping his arms around him.

                         MARTIN
                Mmmmm.... I love your cologne.

                                          FLASHBACK CONTINUES

Todd is standing and smiling down at Martin who closes his eyes and smiles a big, silly, grin. Todd heads out of the kitchen into the living room.

MARTIN
(singing) I'm not Lisa... my name is Julie...

FLASHBACK ENDS

INTERIOR - CHICAGO HOTEL - ROOM

Todd is laying on the bed. He groans and then sits up, kicks off his dress shoes and pulls a pair of jeans, a pullover sweatshirt and boots out of his bags.

CUT TO

INTERIOR - CHICAGO HOTEL - HALLWAY - MOMENTS LATER

Todd exits his hotel room, dressed in the casual attire and carrying his phone and messenger bag. He walks down the hallway, stops at the elevator, presses the DOWN button and waits.

CUT TO

INTERIOR - HOSPITAL - IMAGING ROOM

A Technician and several Doctors are looking over the scans at the injury Martin has sustained. Pointing at clots and discussing diagnosis and possible procedures.

DOCTOR 1
It looks bad. Damn. We need to relieve the swelling immediately, is he prepped?

NURSE 1
Ready,

DOCTOR 2
Has anyone figured out who this guy is? Next of kin or someone contacted? Are we good to go?

NURSE 1
Pulled his ID, according to admitting he actually has some information on file here. Should have some contact information on who can make any major decisions.

The nurse reads over information on Martin's previous hospital visit.

NURSE 1
He's not DNR from any previous visits.

DOCTOR 1
We need to move people, let's go. The group exits the room in a hurry.

Imaging tech types away on the computer from a scan of Martin's ID, entering his name and address, etc.

CUT TO

INTERIOR - HOSPITAL - OPERATING ROOM

Martin is prepped for surgery.

CUT TO

INTERIOR - HOSPITAL - ADMITTING OFFICE

There are a few admins working in the room, they are looking over records from Martin's previous hospital stay,

> ER CLERK 1
>
> Ok, so this guy was admitted for severe bronchitis three years ago. He has an emergency contact. Two actually. One listed as spouse? A guys name? Gross. But there is a family name, sister. "Sandie" let's try giving her a call.

He dials a number, waits for an answer.

> ER CLERK 1
>
> Hello, Captain Adams, this is Richard from ER at Raleigh Memorial. I'm calling regarding the accident victim, Martin Raymond. I have a contact number listed from his previous visit. Listed as his sister, a

Sandie Allen. Address is Morrisville. Will you be making the notification? Great, let me get you the details...

CUT TO

EXTERIOR - CHICAGO - MICHIGAN AVENUE - ROUGHLY SAME TIME

Todd is walking out of an Apple Store with a bag containing his new phone charger. Its cold and he shivers a bit looking up at the sky. Typical winter sky, overcast, there are remnants of snow, now a dirty slush, in places off the street and against buildings.

      TODD
    (to himself) Brrrr chill.

He continues walking down the street. He stops in front of an upscale boutique. He seems lost in thought.

FLASHBACK

EXTERIOR- CHICAGO- LAKE MICHIGAN- 8 YEARS EARLIER- DAYTIME

Todd and Martin are laying in the grass of a park alongside Lake Michigan. There are lots of people walking, biking, playing with dogs. Its a nice warm day.

TODD
So, tell me about your project. Have you always been interested in public art?

MARTIN
(laying back) Yeah, when I was a kid, I loved to color, draw, real crazy imagination. Everyone called me an "artist" but my parents never really looked for ways to foster or support it. They were pretty simple. I guess they thought it would all happen naturally.

TODD
So when did you get into helping others find funding? Why public art?

MARTIN
I dated a guy who was a true artist. All kinds of mediums. He lived check to check. He was good. His stuff should have been in major galleries.

TODD
Why wasn't it?

MARTIN
Oh, he lacked all kinds of ambition. NONE. Pot head, which I am ok with, but he just didn't even think about his future. So I started trying to find grants for him. It isn't easy, but there are ways to get money. I figured if I could find money for him, I could find money for kids, neighborhoods... find ways to bring art to more people.

TODD
Chicago is lousy with it.

MARTIN
AMEN! That's why I love it here! You can't swing a dead cat without hitting a gallery, a statue, a fountain, SOME kind of public art.

TODD
Yah, Desi said you were from the south. Not much art there?

MARTIN
Well, I am from a small Florida town. Miami has lots of stuff, but its not as much classic art. Small museums. Historical for them is the 1920's. IF that. More like the fifties.

Todd laughs. They continue to talk.

FLASHBACK ENDS

EXTERIOR - CHICAGO - MICHIGAN AVENUE - ROUGHLY SAME TIME

Todd is standing in front of a small gallery as his daydream ends. He is smiling. He continues walking down the street, back to his hotel.

CUT TO

INTERIOR - CHICAGO HOTEL - ROOM

Todd enters from the hallway. He flops down in the chair at the desk, pulling the charging cord from the bag and attaching it to his phone. He plugs it into an outlet and we see the phone come slowly to life. It has to reboot.

                              TODD
     (comically dramatic) Arrrrghhh! Tech rage!

Instead, he reaches again for the room phone, dialing out. We hear it go directly to Martin's voice mail.

                              TODD
     HEY! Call me mister. Im leaving in a few for the first
        meeting. BO- ring. Send me a text. X-oh-X.

Todd stretches out and stares at the ceiling a moment, then gets up, opens his suitcase and begins choosing something to wear for the evening.

                                                    CUT TO

INTERIOR - NORTH CAROLINA - HOSPITAL ER - ROUGHLY SAME TIME

A woman comes rushing into the ER and to the admitting desk. She is visibly upset, but not frantic. Her upset appears to us as anger not worry. She knocks on the counter of the admissions desk.

SANDIE
Excuse me!

Two of the busy clerks look over to her, as those sitting at the desks are on the phones, and reviewing computer notices. The ER clerk who spoke with the Police Captain comes over.

ER CLERK 1
Yes, ma'am, how can I...

SANDIE
Look, I don't know who I need to speak with, my brother was in an accident, Martin Raymond. I'm Sandra Allen. I'm his sister. His name is Martin Raymond, M-A-R...

ER CLERK 1
Yes ma'am. Im Richard, I can assist you. First of all, and I apologize, but may I just scan your ID into our visitor system?

Sandie seems irritated, setting her purse down forcefully on the counter and digging through it, pulling out an overstuffed wallet, opening it and showing her ID.

ER CLERK 1
I'm sorry Ms. Allen. Can you remove it and allow me to scan it into our system?

SANDIE
It's MRS. Allen. I'm married.

She pulls the ID from its window slot with a little difficulty and hands it to Richard, who swipes it into the system.

ER CLERK 1
Thank you. (handing it back) Did you speak with Captain Adams? What have you been told?

SANDIE
Martin was in some kind of accident, on his stupid scooter. The police said he was here and in the ICU. What can YOU tell me?

ER CLERK 1
Well, Mrs. Allen, let me get the Doctor for you. All I can tell you is that Martin is in the OR now.

ER CLERK 1 (cont'd)
Let me find you a quiet place to sit, while I let the Doctor know you're here.

SANDIE
Have you called anyone else? Where is his roomma— (pause) His partner?

ER CLERK 1
There was another contact number, but yours was the only one listed as family from his last visit. The sheriff's office sent a deputy out to the address on his drivers license, but from what I understand, there was no one at the residence.

SANDIE
Yah, another contact... that would be "Todd" his boyfriend, or whatever you call it.

ER CLERK 1
Understood. However, I am not in the position to tell you what if anything the Deputy would or would not say to anyone.

SANDIE
Fine, whatever.... I will call him. Who can tell me more RIGHT NOW?

ER CLERK 1
Yes, ma'am. Understood. Calling anyone else will be your decision. Lets wait a moment to see what the doctor can tell us.

SANDIE
How long will that be?

ER CLERK 1
Have a seat right over here, I will find someone now.

Sandie seems more irritated than worried, but follows Richard to a small waiting area away from the main corridor, just off of an office. Richard steps away. Sandie starts rifling through her purse again, pulling out a smart phone, she looks through the numbers and finds a listing she has saved as "Todd A-Hole" and dials it.
We hear a faint beep and voice of Todd's outgoing message. Then, she leaves a message.

                    SANDIE
(stern, almost angry) Hey. It's Sandie. You'd better call me. Please.

                                  CUT TO

INTERIOR - CHICAGO HOTEL - BALLROOM

Todd is mingling with a small group of other professionally dressed folks. Trade show stands and displays are lined against one wall. Waiters pass trays of small elegant hors d'oeuvres. Todd seems interested in the conversation, laughing easily and interjecting here and there. Todd feels something in his pocket and realizes it is his phone leaving a voice message and he excuses himself from the group while he digs it out of his pocket. He sees Sandie's name on the "missed call" screen and he screws up his face in confusion.

                              TODD
            (to others in group) Just a minute folks, if you will
                              excuse me.

Todd steps away while hitting redial.

                              TODD
            (to himself) What the hell does she want now?

Todd listens as Sandie's message plays back. He makes
an irritated face. He dials his phone and we see that it
says "Martin" is who he is calling. Martins voice
message picks up. Todd waits to leave a message.

                              TODD
Hey, listen, your sister is calling me. She sounds PISSED
       about something. Did I miss someones birthday or
  what? Hope you liked the flight info, you wanted a first
    class weekend. I will call her back. Where are you?

Todd pushes button to end call. He gets a slightly
worried look on his face. He dials another number, we
see it says "Sandie."

                                                      CUT TO

INTERIOR - HOSPITAL ER - WAITING ROOM

Sandie now has red eyes from crying, she is pacing a bit,
arms crossed tightly. There is a doctor talking to other

staff in the near background and we overhear a bit.

                    DOCTOR 1
... major contusions, brain swelling, I've just spoken with his sister, although she said she does not have medical directive. Keep an eye on her.

The Doctor walks off and the other staff head off in another direction. Sandie's phone begins to ring.
She sees it says "Todd A-hole" and she pushes the button to answer.

                     SANDIE
          (almost angry) Where are you?

BACK AND FORTH BETWEEN SANDIE AND TODD
INTERIOR - CHICAGO HOTEL - BALLROOM

Todd is off to the side of the crowd, he walks out into a hallway.

                                              CUT TO

INTERIOR - CHICAGO HOTEL - HALLWAY

                      TODD
   (a little put off) Hello to you too, I'm in Chicago....
                working.... why?

                                              CUT TO

INTERIOR - HOSPITAL ER - WAITING ROOM

                    SANDIE
(starts to sob) It's Martin. I don't know.... it's bad.... it was an accident. It's bad.

Sandie breaks down, leaning hard against the wall, she slides down until she is sitting on the floor, even though there are chairs just steps away.

INTERIOR - CHICAGO HOTEL - HALLWAY

Todd looks stricken, his eyes grow wild.

                    TODD
(breathless)What?... what do.... when? Where are you?

                                    CUT TO

INTERIOR - HOSPITAL ER - WAITING ROOM

As the conversation goes back and forth, Sandie is in the hospital ER waiting room, Todd is in the hotel, outside of the ballroom.

                    SANDIE
I'm at the hospital. They called me. The Sheriff did.

Sandie begins to sob a bit, not out of control, but emotional.

> TODD
> Wait, when? What the fuck happened?

> SANDIE
> This afternoon, on his way from school. He was hit by a car. It's bad. He hasn't woken up.

> TODD
> (still in shock) How bad?

Todd starts to walk frantically back and forth in the hallway, almost to the door of the ballroom, changes direction, walking back down the hallway. He stops, reverses and begins to run toward the stairs leading to the main floor.

> SANDIE
> They just said something about brain bleeding, or swelling. They don't know! I don't know! Damn it, that scooter!

Todd reaches the main lobby of the hotel, all the desk clerks are busy, he frantically looks around, notices a valet by the door, runs to him. He covers the phone with his hand.

                           TODD

(to valet) Please, get me a manager right now, I need a
taxi to the airport, I'm going to get my stuff right now.
              Send a manager to room 525.

Todd runs off, still talking into the phone.

                           TODD

I'm coming back right now. I have no idea how. Is he
safe? (voice breaks) I'm coming. Tell me something,
                          Sandie!

Todd runs back to the elevator, as one of the doors open,
he shoves a couple aside, he presses the "5" frantically.

                           TODD
                  (to couple) I'm sorry,

The couple see the frantic look in Todd's face and they
step back as the doors close.

                           TODD
                  Sandie? Hello? Sandie?

The elevator is preventing a decent connection, but he
hears Sandie talking a bit between breaks.

                          SANDIE
He hasn't woken up. They don't know. The doctor just
          said it was bad. They don't know.

The elevator opens on the 5th floor and Todd dashes to his room door, he is fumbling for the key card, struggling to get the door to open and he rushes in.

TODD
Don't lose it, Sandie. I'm checking out and going to the airport right now, I will call you on the way. FIND SOMETHING OUT! OK? Hold on!

SANDIE
OK, I will. (sobs) Todd, you need to fix this.

Sandie hangs up.

CUT TO

INTERIOR - CHICAGO HOTEL - ROOM

Todd looks at the phone as the connection is cut, he is wild eyed. He shoves the phone into his suit coat pocket. He tears around the room, grabbing his belongings, shoving them into the still open suitcase. He bounces back and forth from the bedroom to the bathroom, he spins around, he grabs his coat and scarf, throwing his computer into its bag. There is a knock at the door, Todd swings around. He practically leaps to the door, opening it to one of the Front Desk Managers who looks pleasant but a bit concerned. There is a security officer behind him who leans in to eye Todd.

                    FRONT DESK MANAGER
            Yes sir, Lucas downstairs said you were in need?

The manager sees Todd is dressed in a suit but he is pulling on the last of his winter wear and gathering his bags.

                    FRONT DESK MANAGER
            Is something wrong with the room? How can I help you?

                              TODD
        Listen, I have to leave now, there's an emergency. Just
        close out my room to info on the reservation, can you
                stop a taxi for me? To the airport right now.

The security officer talks into his walkie-talkie, it beeps twice as his call is going through

                        HOTEL SECURITY
        Yeah, its George, listen, get me a taxi right now, on hold,
                        taking passenger to...

The three exit into the hallway, the Manager runs ahead to press the elevator button.

                              TODD
                             O'Hare

                        HOTEL SECURITY
            ...to O'Hare. Coming down now. Bill it to hotel.

FRONT DESK MANAGER
Thank you George. (to Todd) We can use the card on file for the room, don't worry. Is there anyone we can call?

TODD
No, no. Wait, yes, can you get ahold of Eric Boswell, he is chairing the conference in Ballroom.... shit... Ballroom...

FRONT DESK MANAGER
I can find it, Eric Boswell. Whats the message?

The elevator arrives, it is going up, the Security Guard enters a key into the control panel and presses the Lobby button as Todd and the Manager enter. Another guest looks on confused.

HOTEL SECURITY
Sorry sir, slight lobby detour.

TODD
Just tell him that I had to leave. Tell him anything.

FRONT DESK MANAGER
Certainly. Is there any other luggage?

TODD
This is it. I'm an expert at packing, didn't you know? (he laughs a bit nervously)

The elevator opens onto a semi busy lobby and Todd rushes to the front entrance. The Hotel Security makes a motion behind him, indicating to the valet that this is the passenger for the taxi. Todd rushes out and the valet opens the taxi door, Todd throws his bags into it and turns.

                    TODD
Listen, thanks. (to driver) Please drive safely, but get me to the airport as quickly as you can.

He doesn't wait for a response from Front Desk Manager but closes the door behind him, struggling to retrieve his phone from his suit coat as the taxi heads off.

INTERIOR - CHICAGO CAB -

It has begun snowing, and Todd just looks out of the window as the taxi makes its way into traffic. He closes his eyes.

                                    FLASHBACK

INTERIOR - SANDIE'S HOME - 8 YEARS AGO - EVENING

There is a small group of ladies having a baby shower at Sandie's home for one of her friends. Martin and Todd walk through the living room where the group is assembled.

The ladies, who had been talking animatedly, quiet a bit as the two walk through. Kamille, a light skinned woman of color, seems to be the one actually throwing the shower.

                    KAMILLE
    Oh, look, Sandie's handsome brother!

                    MARTIN
    Hey Kamille. Great shower. Congratulations Denise.

                    TODD
Yes, Denise, nice to have met you, sorry about crashing through your shower. Congrats.

Denise is the pregnant woman, for whom the shower is being given. She is seated in a large chair, surrounded by gifts, a few streamers, and a few stuffed animals, all with pastel colors ablaze. She seems to force a smile.

                    DENISE
    Sure, thanks. OK girls, lets have cake.

                    KAMILLE
Martin, I guess this is something you can only enjoy from the outside... as a man, I mean.

She says it playfully, but there is a slight hint of malice in her tone.

MARTIN
Not true! We threw an awesome shower for our friends
Holly and Delores for their first, didn't we Todd?

TODD
(apprehensively) Yeah, it was very nice. They had
a little boy... Martin, let's go.

KAMILLE
Yeah well,

SANDIE
Listen everyone, Martin was just leaving. He and Todd
have their own things to do....

MARTIN
Thanks sis. Sure, congratulations again Denise.

KAMILLE
I guess you won't be a dad though, will you Martin? Or a
mother? Sorry, not sure which of you... is...

Now the malice is clear. Martin stiffens a bit. Todd looks
like he is getting angrier.

TODD
Let's go Martin, let's go.

SANDIE

Oh, he is an OK uncle though. The kids seem to like staying with him. (nervous laughter)

KAMILLE

You let him watch your kids?

The room goes silent.

SANDIE

Kamille, he is a great uncle to my kids. And I have learned to accept him for who he...

MARTIN

(quietly) "Accept" me?

TODD

(concerned) Martin...

MARTIN

"Acceptance" isn't "love." "Acceptance" isn't what makes a family.

SANDIE

(flustered) Marty please. (to Kamille) Kamille, stop. I respect your... I mean, I understand why you....

MARTIN

You DO? What is there to understand?

KAMILLE
I just think "traditional" marriage is what makes a family.

TODD
Martin, please, c'mon.

MARTIN
"Traditional marriage?" Aren't you on your third? Lucky for you, I guess.

KAMILLE
Fine then, marriage as ordained by...

MARTIN
Don't EVEN try and say "God" or the Bible. According to the Bible, your tribe could trade you off as soon as you bled, for livestock. THAT was marriage in the Bible.

TODD
Martin! Now! I'm ready to go.

MARTIN
Sandie, your kids are my family. (controlling himself) But Todd is my family. He is YOUR family. I don't debate beliefs, but my family will be respected in your house. You decide.

Martin turns to Denise.

MARTIN
Denise, forgive me. This party is for you. (to Sandie) Sis, thanks. Sorry we barged through.

Martin turns to Kamille

MARTIN
You know, you were born before 1968 right? Loving vs. Virginia. Look it up, it wasn't so long ago your parents were treated the way you choose to treat me.

Sandie looks very irritated. She pulls Todd slightly aside, speaks quietly, directly to him.

SANDIE
You need to fix this! He's acting this way because of you. He's not some kind of protester.

TODD
I don't control him! I want him to stop too. This isn't MY influence.

SANDIE
Yes it is. This is all about you. He's defending YOU. Just fix this!

Todd looks at Sandie a bit confused. He doesn't see the connection.

                    MARTIN
                Fine, let's go.

Martin and Todd leave.

                              FLASHBACK ENDS

INTERIOR - CHICAGO CAB

Todd rubs his temples. The cab is still en route to the airport, the snow is barely coming down, there are still lots of cars on the road. Todd holds up his phone and hits dial to Sandie. Her voice is heard on the phone.

                    SANDIE
                Todd? (she sounds tired)

                    TODD
                OK, what can you tell me. How bad?

INTERIOR - HOSPITAL - ROOM

Sandie is standing against the wall, Martin is in a large bed, head wrapped, breathing tubes and IV lines, as well as monitors are everywhere. There are two medical staff by his bed. Sandie looks completely exhausted.

Sandie is in hospital room and Todd in the cab.

SANDIE
He is out of surgery. They don't know. They are still here in the room. He is still out. Coma or something. Do they do that to him? Im waiting for more information. I don't know what to do.

TODD
Where are the kids?

SANDIE
Ed has them. I told him to keep them away. Not like this.

TODD
How bad was the accident? Why a coma? Was he hit?

SANDIE
From what the sheriff told me, someone said he was run off the side of the road and then bounced into oncoming traffic. Someone couldn't stop. They were not going too fast, but it was still bad. Somehow his helmet came off. Broken rib, broken finger, but it's all how he hit. or how he was hit. His head...

TODD
(voice chokes) Will he make it?

SANDIE
Todd, I don't know. I'm sorry. I love him, I do. (grits her teeth) I'm sorry, but for some reason I just hate you right now.

TODD
Sandie... I can't lose him. (he grimaces as he holds back a choked sob) You have to help me here.

SANDIE
He has barely spoken to me in over a year. Why did you keep him from me?

TODD
Sandie, listen, please, just let me get there.

The two medical staff whisper to each other, one comes over and gently touches Sandie's arm.

SANDIE
Todd, hold on,

Sandie drops the phone to her side, her arms still crossed tightly.

DOCTOR 1
Ma'am, it's not good. The bleeding hasn't stopped completely, the swelling is still critical. We may need to take him back into surgery. I'll be right back. Please, sit here for a moment, I will bring in his belongings.

SANDIE
I don't need his STUFF!

The Doctor seems to understand, as Sandie slumps into a chair near a long sill by the window. The doctor leaves. Sandie looks at the phone, it still says "Todd A-hole" and she sobs. She puts the phone to her ear.

> SANDIE
> Did you hear that?

> TODD
> Only barely. What more surgery?

> SANDIE
> I am guessing on his brain. Bleeding and swelling. Dammit Todd...

An aide brings in Martin's messenger bag and his clothing in a plastic bag.

> SANDIE
> Great, they give me his stuff.

> TODD
> Just hang in there. I'm almost to the airport, let me call you right back. Do you have video calling?

> SANDIE
> What? What....

> TODD
> Facetime, Skype, some kind of video conference...

                    SANDIE
I have an iPhone, thats on there right? The kids use it I
                     know.

                     TODD
I am going to call on FaceTime in a moment then, can
you hold it so I can see him? Just as soon as I get into
               the airport, OK? Please.

                    SANDIE
                Fine...but Todd?

                     TODD
                     yes?

                    SANDIE
              PLEASE. say a prayer?

Sandie ends the call

                                                  CUT TO

INTERIOR - CHICAGO CAB
CONTINUOUS

Todd looks at the phone, as the call is disconnected. He
keeps his teeth clenched, holding back emotion, as the
screen goes dark. He closes his eyes tightly and stiffens.

                                                  CUT TO

EXTERIOR - CHICAGO HIGHWAY OUT OF THE CITY
CONTINUOUS

The cab is in traffic, the airport in the near distance, traffic flowing as the snow is falling, only slightly heavier.

INTERIOR - HOSPITAL - ROOM
CONTINOUS

Sandie walks over to Martin, she reaches out as if to touch his arm, but cannot. She steps back a bit, then picks up the plastic bag containing his clothing, sets it aside. She pulls out his messenger bag, returns to the chair, pulling it a little closer to the bed. It has dirt and gravel on it, it seems a bit banged up from the accident. She opens it. It has a paperback copy of "The Little Prince," a notebook, a small brown bottle. Sandie looks at the bottle, it says "Todd" on it, she removes the cap and smells it...

                                          FLASHBACK

INTERIOR - TODD AND MARTINS HOME - LIVING ROOM
SEVERAL YEARS EARLIER

Todd, Martin, Sandie, a few other folks who are obviously friends of Todd's and Martin, are all gathered in the living room. There are some open gifts laying around, a few T-shirts, a new pair of high-top Converse shoes, a signed concert mini-poster of Cyndi Lauper.

Martin has just finished opening a gift and everyone is laughing and cheering. Sandie is enjoying herself, but looks slightly uncomfortable in the mix of the hip, artsy, crowd. There is a lesbian couple, three single gay men and a straight couple and Sandie. She forces a smile.

> SANDIE
> Wow, quite a haul, Marty. I didn't realize you were so into coffee?

Sandie holds up a ceramic coffee mug with a fun slogan on it.

> MARTIN
> Life's blood sis.

> SANDIE
> ...and more T-shirts, obviously.

> MARTIN
> I am pretty easy to shop for. BUT....

Martin pulls a small box from under the coffee table, opens it. It is filled with several small brown bottles, each has a label with a name on it.

> MARTIN
> A good host always has a small gift for his guests and even though it's my birthday, these are for you guys.

Martin begins to hand them out. They are essential oil mixes, everyone opens theirs and smells them, all smiling and agreeing how great the scents are.

                         SANDIE
               Wait, there are two "TODD"s here.

                         MARTIN
                   I know. One is mine.

Martin hands one to Todd, who smiles a huge smile.

                          TODD
                     My personal one?

                         MARTIN
     It was the same one I made for you for our anniversary.
       You thought I had forgotten about them, didn't you?

                          TODD
                    It has been a while.

Todd opens it and smells it, closes his eyes a moment.

                          TODD
              Why the extra bottle of "Todd?"

                         MARTIN
    For me. It's what I will wear from now on. It's a way of
                 staying connected vibrationally.

Martin leans in and gently punches Todd on the arm. Then hugs him.

                  TODD
    Wait, everyone, I have one more for him.

Everyone returns to their seats.

                MARTIN
    You sly dog... after Cyndi Lauper, what is there?

Todd goes to a drawer in a curio, pulls a small blue Tiffany box, leans in and kisses Martin on the forehead and hands him the box. Several guests make remarks.

                GUEST 1
    oooh... Tiffany.

                GUEST 2
    Somebody's knocking it later...

                GUEST 3
    Gays...

The guests all laugh.

Martin opens the box. Its a stylish, classic, "RETURN TO TIFFANYS" key chain with a single key on it. It looks like an old house key.

MARTIN
What's this to?

TODD
That, is the key to the apartment I had in Chicago, when we first met.

MARTIN
You don't own that, do you?

TODD
No. But for the year we dated there, before I got the job offer, I wanted to ask you every weekend to just stay with me. To move in. I dreaded every morning that I packed my duffel and left. My room mate never allowed us privacy, and I didn't know how to ask her to leave. But if I could do it again, I would have asked you on our second date...

GUEST 3
sheesh... like a couple of LESBIANS.

The crowd laughs softly, but they are also moved.
Martin has a tear in his eye.

TODD
... I would have told you that I knew. I knew. I've always known.

Martin gets up, holds the key ring up as it shines in the light, the one old key in stark contrast. He wraps his arms around Todd.

> MARTIN
> (whispering to Todd) I love you. Really, really. Someday, you're gonna marry me.

Sandie overhears this last part and gets a slightly shocked look on her face.

> FLASHBACK ENDS

INTERIOR - HOSPITAL - ROOM
CONTINOUS

Sandie is holding both the small brown bottle and an obviously used Tiffany keyring. It still has just the one key on it.

> CUT TO

EXTERIOR - CHICAGO - OHARE - SAME EVENING

Todd is exiting the cab, he starts to fumble in his pocket.

> CABBIE
> It's cool man, the hotel picked it up. You...

Todd finds a twenty dollar bill in his pocket and hands it to the driver.

                    TODD
                    Thanks,

Todd doesn't wait for a response, but hoists one bag over his shoulder and extends the handle on the other, pulling it behind him, he dodges others waiting and walking about in the departing flights area. The airport is busy with normal activity.

                                        CUT TO

INTERIOR - CHICAGO - OHARE
CONTINUOUS

Todd searches for the right counter for his airline, it has a long line, he spies an airline rep walking about answering questions, he approaches her. She is dark haired, exotic, Indian heritage.

          AIRLINE REPRESENTATIVE
    (to a passenger) No sir, the delays are pretty minor.

                  PASSENGER
    This sucks. This is why I live in Florida. All the delays
           start up north, thanks for nothing.

Passenger drags his over-sized bag, as he storms off. The Airline Representative turns to see Todd approaching. She seems frustrated, but adjusts herself and forces a smile.

> AIRLINE REPRESENTATIVE
> Yes sir, will you be flying with us this evening?

> TODD
> Listen, I don't know how to do this, my flight isn't until tomorrow, no... wait, Sunday, but there has been an accident and I need to fly back as soon as possible.

The Airline Representative looks at Todd, noticing that he is obviously distressed. She is concerned.

> AIRLINE REPRESENTATIVE
> I'm so sorry, come with me.

She leads Todd over to an empty station beyond the stanchions of the other passengers waiting in line. Some see Todd being helped and make signs of frustration.

> AIRLINE REPRESENTATIVE
> Please just hand me your ID, do you happen to have your boarding pass for Sunday?

> TODD
> I do, somewhere, I don't know, it's.... here, here's my license...

AIRLINE REPRESENTATIVE
(typing into the computer) This should do, yes, here. OK, the next flight to RDU is a bit delayed, so not expected until 8:35. Minor delays, just on some inbound, weather related, but no cancellations at this point. But no connection, it's direct, non-stop.

Todd seems lost, unable to think or make a decision.

TODD
What do you think? Is that it?

AIRLINE REPRESENTATIVE
I'm checking our partner carriers, nothing that could potentially put you there any earlier, I'm afraid.

She looks at Todd sympathetically. He looks like he might not be able to stand much longer.

AIRLINE REPRESENTATIVE
Listen, let's change your booking now, with the delays, I don't want you to lose this seat.

TODD
um...yeah.... thanks.... um... what do I need? Let me get my card...

Todd again fumbles for his wallet, grasping his cell phone tightly.

                    AIRLINE REPRESENTATIVE
You were upgraded, it was complimentary it seems and you are Premium Passenger status, it wont be necessary. You're all set. I don't mean to pry, but do you need a place to sit? Out of the crowd?

                              TODD
             Thanks. No, I mean yes. Yes, please.

She again leads Todd away from the check-in area as some of the passengers still waiting groan audibly. They walk a short distance to the security checkpoint, she motions for a TSA agent, who comes over and she whispers in his ear. Todd is frantically trying to empty his pockets into the bowl in the TSA agents extended hand. The Airline Rep takes his bag and hands them off to another TSA agent at the X-ray, while the first TSA excuses himself in the waiting line, ushering Todd through. Todd is oblivious to some of the stares of the line of waiting passengers. After the requisite check point activities, the Airline Rep ushers him to a phone on a column, she dials.

                    AIRLINE REPRESENTATIVE
Hey Steven, this is Jasmin, I'm sending a gentleman to you, please escort him to the private lounge. Thanks. (pause) no, nothing major, just the normal "I hate Chicago weather" issues. I'll keep you posted.

She hangs up, turns to Todd.

                    AIRLINE REPRESENTATIVE
You are all set, it's none of my business, but you seem
   pretty upset, if you need anything at all, tell them
             Jasmin said to call with any issues.

Todd looks at her, holding it together.

                    AIRLINE REPRESENTATIVE
Look for Steven at your gate, he will set you up in an
                area out of the main crowd.

                              TODD
        I really cant thank you enough. Thank you.

                    AIRLINE REPRESENTATIVE
                  Namaste, I wish you well.

She smiles and turns to leave. Todd watches her leave.
He is lost in thought again, as he heads toward his gate.

                                                    FLASHBACK

EXTERIOR - CHICAGO - OUTSIDE PARK AREA -
SPRING - DAY

Todd is sitting on a bench, he has a street bike by his
side. Martin comes walking up, a bit sweaty, with a yoga
mat in a carrier, drinking from a large bottle of water.
He is wearing a novelty T-shirt with "Namaste" on it.

TODD
"Namaste" what's that?

MARTIN
It's a traditional greeting, "I bow to you."

Martin holds his hands together in front of his heart and does a slight bow.

TODD
Really?

MARTIN
Really really. Translations can be more flowery, but its how you honor the other person, no matter what.

TODD
Even if they're assholes?

MARTIN
Especially then. I'm not great at it, trust me.

TODD
Just what religion are you?

MARTIN
None. All. I don't know. Blah blah blah. (air quotes) "I'm not religious, I'm just spiritual." You know. Peace, love, Joni Mitchell. I don't know.

TODD
Wow, it kind of rains cats and dogmas with you....

Martin gives him a comic roll of the eyes...

TODD
... Still, sounds better than what I was thinking. A better way to believe, I guess.

MARTIN
Oh, I am not interested in being better than anyone else. Just better than who I was last year, or yesterday.

TODD
Still seems like a lot of work. (laughs) Kidding, thats cool. I don't really have a personal belief.

MARTIN
Well, you believe in something, whatever it is. God, physics, METAphysics. Oprah.

TODD
Name dropper. There ya go. Let's change the subject.

MARTIN
One last question for you to consider, W W J A D?

TODD
Huh?

                    MARTIN
            What would Julie Andrews do?

They both laugh.

                              FLASHBACK ENDS

INTERIOR - AIRPORT
CONTINUOUS

Todd is approaching his gate, he double checks the boarding pass. There is a small queue of passengers, again waiting. Todd stays back a moment. A young man walks by the gate counter, his name tag says Steven. Todd waves, hesitantly, to get his attention. Steven notices, holds his hand up, as if to indicate he needs just a moment, speaks with the counter agent, then comes over to Todd.

                    STEVEN
    Are you the gentleman that Jamin assisted? She said
    you need a quiet place to sit? Did you need an outlet for
                    anything?

Todd realized that he is asking in case he needed to plug in a phone or a computer, which gives him a thought.

                    TODD
            Yes, that would be fantastic...

Todd looks around, wondering if there is a break room nearby.

                    STEVEN
            We do have a lounge area here.

Steve extends his arm in gracious way of escorting Todd across the aisle, where there is a frosted glass door.

                    STEVEN
                 Just in here.

                                            CUT TO

INTERIOR - AIRPORT - LOUNGE - CONTINUOUS

Steven opens the door, there is an empty desk with a phone and a clean, simple but stylish lounge area, currently empty.

                    STEVEN
    I apologize, due to some of the delays, its kind of "all
    hands on deck" out there right now. I can call for
    someone to get you a beverage, if you like. There are
    outlets on either side, but wifi reception for me is a bit
                better nearer the windows.

                     TODD
    That's perfect, thanks. Nothing to drink, thank you.

Steven reaches behind another counter and produces two small bottles of water, sets them onto a small table near the window seating.

> STEVEN
> Just in case.

> TODD
> Thanks. When do you anticipate boarding for....

Todd checks his boarding pass and hands it to Steven.

> STEVEN
> OK, this flight hasn't had any further delays, its en route. We should make an announcement soon as to updates, you will hear the announcements here. Are you all set? I should get back out there. This phone (indicates the one on the desk at the entry) will ring us at the gate, by pressing 212. Just think "New York" and ask for Steven.

> TODD
> Thanks again.

Steven exits out of the lounge.

Todd takes a deep breath, opens one of the bottles of water and downs it quickly, then replaces the cap. He opens the second, taking one drink. He retrieves his phone from his jacket and dials Sandie.

SANDIE
Todd?

TODD
Hey... um.... I'm afraid to ask anything.

SANDIE
No change yet. Nothing. They come in, look and they go. It doesn't even sound like he is breathing.

TODD
Please, don't say things like that. On your phone, I assume there is a camera. When I click over to video phone, can you point it at him?

CUT TO

INTERIOR - HOSPITAL - ROOM
CONTINOUS

SANDIE
Why do you want to see him like this?

Back and forth between Sandie and Todd shows Sandie in hospital room and Todd in the airport lounge.

TODD
I just want to see him. And I want him to hear me too.

Sandie does not seem to realize Todd's own desperation.

> SANDIE
> He's not awake!

> TODD
> He could still hear me. Sandie please. I need your help here.

> SANDIE
> What do I do?

> TODD
> I am just going to switch to video....

Todd presses the button on his phone to switch to video call,

> TODD
> (to himself) C'mon, c'mon

We see a picture of Todd appear on Sandie's phone, and vice versa.

> SANDIE
> Ok, now what? Do you see me? You look awful.

> TODD
> Just turn the camera so I can see him. Turn the phone.

Sandie turns the phone so that the image on Todd's phone spins and then settles on Martin, laying in the hospital bed. Todd breaks, nearly dropping the phone, running his free hand through his hair. He sobs a bit.

TODD
(between sobs) Oh baby. Martin.... Martin.

He continues to choke out a few unintelligible words, forces himself into an upright position and looks again at the image of Martin.

TODD
Listen, I love you. I love you. Stay with me, please. I'm coming. I'm on my way. Don't go. Please, just don't go. Hear me, Martin. Listen to me. You are my family.

Back in the hospital room, Sandie's face is set almost unemotional. She listens to Todd talk to Martin, she starts to shake, collapsing into the chair, dropping the phone to her side. On Todd's phone he sees the screen shake and then all he can see is Sandie's shoes.

TODD
Sandie! Sandie!

SANDIE
(sobbing) I'm his family. I'm his family too. I didn't mean it. I didn't.

Sandie gasps a few more times then puts the phone back up so that she sees Todd.

SANDIE
I cant. He cant..... Todd, ...I ... I'm sorry. I never meant to hurt either of you. I don't understand... you. I don't understand the two of you. We weren't raised with...

TODD
Sandie, enough! I didn't blame you. Martin didn't blame you. That's done. Please, put the phone back next to him. Wait, did they bring you his bag?

SANDIE
Yeah, it's here, it's ok.

TODD
Is his iPad in there?

Sandie goes to the messenger bag again, opens it, finds Martin's computer case and a small iPad case.

SANDIE
Why does he have two? Doesn't he know that your bag shouldn't weigh more than 5 pounds? (she laughs and sobs all together)

TODD
Does it work? Is it on?

Sandie presses the home button and the screen comes to life, showing an older photo of Todd holding a small black and white kitten. She swipes the screen and the number pad comes up.

      SANDIE
  Yeah, it's working. Do you know his password?

      TODD
  Its either 5683 or 8633. Try those.

Sandie punches in 5683 and the image shakes to indicate an incorrect password attempt. She then types in 8633 and it works. The screen comes to life with a different picture of Martin and Todd, with their arms around a tree, not quite touching.

      SANDIE
    Yeah, 8633 worked.

Todd half smiles and half grimaces again with emotion.

      TODD
  (to himself) 8-6-3-3. T-O-D-D.

      SANDIE
    Now what?

      TODD
  First, go to settings, first screen.

                    SANDIE
                    OK. Got it.

                    TODD
        Go to Cellular Data, turn that on.

Sandie swipes and chooses icon to turn on cellular data.

                    SANDIE
                    OK.

                    TODD
Back on home screen. Look for the icon for Face Time, its just like one we are using now, set his iPad up so that I can see him, the smaller pic in the upper corner will be what I see, when I call in, OK?

                    SANDIE
        You are going to hang up with me?

                    TODD
Just briefly, then I will dial in to his iPad. OK? If theres an issue, I'm calling you right back.

                    SANDIE
                    OK.

Todd disconnects the call. He sees his battery is low again on his phone.

                    TODD
                   DAMMIT!

Todd searches his computer case for the phone charging cord he recently purchased, plugging it in to the outlet by the table, hearing the beep of the connection.

                                        CUT TO

INTERIOR - HOSPITAL - ROOM

Sandie is setting up the iPad as it makes a ringing noise, she sees it indicates Todd is calling in. She presses the screen to accept the call, Todd's face fills the largest portion of the screen and she sees herself in the upper corner.

                   SANDIE
          Where are you? Why is it so dark?

Todd looks around, it is still darkened in the lounge. Just before he speaks an announcement is made referencing his flight. It is expected to land shortly.

                    TODD
    Airport. In a lounge, waiting for my flight. Should be here in a few, hopefully take off just after. Can you turn it so I can see him?

Sandie turns the iPad around, setting it on a bedside tray that was set off to the side, adjusting it so that its case becomes a stand and she checks to see that the small image is of Martin in the bed.

TODD
He looks so small.

SANDIE
What are those terms? Could he die? He just looks banged up, except for the big bandage on his head and scrapes, I've seen worse from a soccer game.

TODD
Brain damage is bad, Sandie. Did they give you ANY indication of prognosis?

SANDIE
Evidently they just want him to not have to go back into surgery. They come in and out of here every....

As Sandie is talking, another orderly walks in, solemn.

ORDERLY
Excuse me, Mrs.... Allen?

SANDIE
Yes.

ORDERLY
The doctor wanted me to know if you needed to look over any....

The orderly notices the iPad.

ORDERLY
Excuse me, who is this? (indicating Todd)

SANDIE
This is Todd. He is my brother's friend. I mean, my brothers...

TODD
Husband.

ORDERLY
I see.... well, Mrs. Allen you are the closest family member...

TODD
No. She's not. I am. We both are.

ORDERLY
I understand sir, however, in North Carolina...

TODD
(livid) I don't know you, but watch your step. I'm going to be IN this conversation!

SANDIE
Please, it's OK. Just tell us.

ORDERLY
Well, its just, the Doctor wanted to know if you needed to look over these.... forms... to ascertain a direction in the event a decision... I'm sorry. Sir, might you have a durable power of attorney or medical Advance Directive to make any decisions involving end of life..

TODD
JUST SHUT UP! Don't say it!

Sandie gets up and gets the iPad, holding it so that Todd is now seeing her.

SANDIE
Todd.... (turns to orderly) excuse me, ma'am, is there a reason to discuss this now?! What the hell are the doctors not telling us?

ORDERLY
Your brothers injuries are very serious. We don't have any directive on file. It's important there is a clear decision maker and legally the hospital needs....

Todd is speechless. Sandie stands up.

SANDIE
We will make any decisions as a family. Whatever my brothers husband needs to do, we will do. Now, unless you have some function to perform, get a doctor in here.

ORDERLY
Certainly, maybe you can discuss with the doctor who has the authority the hospital needs.

SANDIE
JUST GO.

The orderly looks at the monitor and respirator briefly, then leaves.

TODD
Sandie, listen. Let's not fight between us. I have to trust you, too. Wait a moment.

An announcement is made indicating Todd's flight is inbound and will be at the gate soon.

TODD
… OK, great. The plane is here. Give me half an hour to be in the air. I should be there in a few hours, if no delay. How's your weather?

SANDIE
Cold, misty. No issues, I'd think.

                           TODD
Can you turn the iPad to him a few minutes more? I just
                      want to see him.

The iPad beeps, indicates a low battery.

                          SANDIE
It just beeped. Says low battery. I didn't see the
                         charger...

                           TODD
Just give me a moment. Turn it towards him. I'll call you
                    back as soon as I can.

Sandie turns the iPad back to face Martin, setting it on the bed table.

Todd looks at Martin, silent. He is frustrated, stricken, but his face regains a calm demeanor. He rubs his eyes, but wont look away.

                           TODD
              (almost silently) Hang on baby.

Sandie is positioned so that she can see a bit of Todd in the iPad and she watches the monitors as they record and display information she is oblivious to. She looks over Martin's body and cannot discern a rise and fall of his breath.

SANDIE
(almost silently as well) I'm sorry Martin.... so sorry.

FLASHBACK

INTERIOR - COFFEE HOUSE - SEVERAL YEARS EARLIER - DAYTIME

Martin and Sandie are seated together.

SANDIE
I can't believe you brought your own mug.

MARTIN
Do you know how many cups are thrown away every day, just from coffee?

SANDIE
Ugh. Another crusade.

MARTIN
I'm not asking YOU to do anything differently. You made the comment. Anyway, what are you guys visiting here? Why didn't you tell me before last night?

SANDIE
Ed was offered a job here. A good one. Research Triangle something or other. They want him to be a project leader.

MARTIN
WOW, what kind of project?

SANDIE
How the hell should I know?

MARTIN
Don't... (laughing) Don't you know what your husband does? He's a reporting and analyst specialist for a big Pharma company.)

SANDIE
Yeah, but I don't know what he does.

Martin laughs again.

SANDIE
Do you know what Todd does?

MARTIN
Yes, as a matter of fact, he is a marketing and branding strategist.

SANDIE
Well, hooray. Another reason you're better.

MARTIN
Are you mad at something?

SANDIE

Look, I'm not sure I want to move here. It wasn't certain until just yesterday. I didn't want to alarm you unnecessarily.

MARTIN

(laughing) Ha! Why wouldn't I want you to be closer? I can see the kids grow up.

SANDIE

I've done a lot of.... growing... since you and Todd.... got together. But you know Ed. He's still kinda punchy about it. I'm not so sure he'd welcome a.....closer....relationship.

MARTIN

The kids love me. I love them. If you want to let him keep your family apart, just sneak them over from time to time. I'm done fighting willfully ignorant people. Certainly not looking for it. What do you think though? I'm not looking for your "understanding" or your "acceptance." Todd stood by me, he didn't judge me or leave me after finding out....

Martin stops himself.

MARTIN

... never mind. Listen. You and the kids are all I have as far as "blood" relations.

SANDIE
Oh please, there are a hundred cousins in West Virginia alone...

MARTIN
Sorry, they don't count. I could walk by them in the street and we wouldn't know each other. You know what I mean. Since mom died, you have been distant. If you are going to live in the same town as me, you will have to decide to either see me or ignore me. Its big, but it isn't New York. We ran into each other a lot in Chicago without planning it, this town is a bit smaller.

SANDIE
Well, thats just it. The last time we were in the same town, it wasn't great.

MARTIN
Hey, they're your friends.

SANDIE
I won't have any friends here. Most people we will know at first will be Ed's work people. I'm tired of men in one room, wives in the other.

MARTIN
Ugh. Do you hear yourself? "Men" and "wives?" why are you defining yourself as HIS wife? You had a great career in Chicago. There's plenty you could do here. Let it be the WOMEN in one room and HUSBANDS in the

other, if not MEN and WOMEN in the same room? Why did gay folks get called "queer?" Straight people are more "queer" than we are....

SANDIE
How can you use that word? Isn't that hate speech?

MARTIN
NOT if I say it. It takes the sting out. Like "WOMYN" with a "Y." It's empowering! Like, if you spelled it "K-U-N-T." Sandie gasps but laughs despite herself.

SANDIE
That word is just awful! No matter HOW its spelled.

MARTIN
OK. Sure. We're off topic. I'd be happy to have you in the same city, back in my life. I don't love you because we're related. I love you because you climbed trees with me. I love you through the death of our parents. I love you because you let me cry when Jimbo seduced me in ninth grade and ignored me in tenth. You knew before I did. I don't know what changed.

SANDIE
Well, I may not love Todd, but I do love you. He just makes me feel... I don't know... unworthy somehow. Like I don't deserve his friendship.

MARTIN
Todd is one of the most noble men I have ever met. He would welcome you as a sister-in-law. But he wont compromise. That's one of the reasons I happen to love HIM. It took him a while to even "come out" but he is his own man.

SANDIE
What do you mean?

MARTIN
He's just... private. Didn't go to bars. Didn't have a lot of "out" friends. His college life and corporate life was pretty conservative.

SANDIE
Was he out to his own family?

MARTIN
He doesn't have any family at all, blood I mean. He was a foster kid through High School. ...Didn't keep in contact with any of his fosters. He doesn't have anyone he looks back on. He might not even need me. But he LOVES me. Get it?

SANDIE
Love. How do you know he loves you?

TODD
You wanna know why I REALLY believe it?

SANDIE
(curious) Yeah....

MARTIN
I know because he has seen me almost fall apart and he doesn't try to make it better.

SANDIE
That doesn't make sense. Wouldn't he TRY and make things better.

MARTIN
He knows he can't. He knows that there is a deep sadness in me that I will never get rid of. The kind of sadness that doesn't cripple me, but never the less reasserts itself from time to time, to let me know that I'm... wounded.

SANDIE
(concerned) You mean you still have... have you tried again... I mean....?

MARTIN
No. But he's woken up when I'm whimpering and crying in my sleep and he doesn't try to say things that he knows can't help. I woke up once, knowing that I was having the dreams again and he was just holding my hand. He didn't ask for explanation, he just sat there, looking at me. He didn't tell me things were "OK" or "not

to worry." He let it hurt. And by not fighting it, I am able to let it pass.

SANDIE
Does he know... did you tell him that you tried...

MARTIN
I don't know if he knows that. But he knows me. He won't walk out of the room in an argument. He doesn't try to hurt me when he is hurt. He'd let me fall apart and stand there with nothing but love in his eyes. Love, is not what people say, it's what they DO. Love is a verb. It's what you do when you DON'T feel it and it's how you remind yourself that it's real when you can feel it.

Sandie is quiet, looking at what is left of her coffee.

SANDIE
Marty, you know I love you too, right?

MARTIN
I do.

Martin reaches out and holds up his thumb. Sandie hesitates a moment, but reaches up her thumb and presses it to Martin's.

MARTIN
You willing to believe that he loves me too?

Martin leans in and bumps shoulders with his sister. He is smiling gently.

SANDIE

Yeah, I guess so. Just don't tell him that. When Im ready, tell him I will make him some cookies. That'll be the sign. Then we'll be family.

TODD

Hey, I know a great couple of lesbo Realtors who can help you find a new home.

SANDIE

Baby steps. Baby steps.

FLASHBACK ENDS

INTERIOR - HOSPITAL - ROOM

Sandie sits back in the chair.

Todd hears his flight arrival announcement.

TODD

Hey, my plane is here. I'm not sure how crowded it's going to be, I am going to get seated. When the doctor comes in, stand your ground. Get some answers. I will get a cab to the hospital. I will call you as soon as we land. And Sandie, talk to him. Tell him you're there. Tell him I'm coming.

SANDIE
Yeah, I will. Todd... Thanks. And can you do me a favor?

TODD
Yeah,

SANDIE
Just keep praying.

TODD
I will do whatever it takes.

SANDIE
See you soon.

Todd signs off the iPad, gathers his bags and heads out of the lounge, just as Steven was coming back in.

STEVEN
Oh, good. I was just coming to check on you. Flight is full, two on standby. First class is boarding in a moment.

TODD
Thanks, thanks again.

They exit the lounge.

INTERIOR - AIRPORT - TERMINAL
CONTINUOUS

Steven heads off toward the gate without looking back. Todd negotiates through the crowd of straggling passengers exiting flights and those who begin to crowd the gate for departure. He maneuvers to an area close to the gate, eyeing other passengers. Still mostly singles and couples, only three young children that he can see. He hears Sandies voice in his head.

                    SANDIE
            (VO) Just keep praying.

Todd rubs his eyes again.

                    TODD
        (whispers) God, please. Just.... please.

An announcement is made for first class passengers and Todd advances to the gate, Steven is there. Todd shows him the boarding pass and his ID, he shrugs as it seems redundant but must be done. Steven nods and keeps the line moving. Todd takes long strides down the gantry to the door of the plane. Normal pleasantries from these Flight Attendants, Todd is ushered to the first row in First Class again.

                                        CUT TO

INTERIOR - AIRPLANE - FIRST CLASS CABIN
CONTINOUS

He puts carry-on in overhead and takes his seat. He takes his phone and switches it to "airplane mode" and after, he begins scrolling through myriad apps on his phone. Passengers continue to fill the plane, attendants ready for take off. Some announcements are made. All passengers are seated and the attendants start the safety video, they ready the plane for take off. The plane begins to back out of the gate and taxi as they finish their duties, Todd is lost in his phone until the call to turn it off. He does so and just rests his head against the window.

                                                    DISSOLVE

INTERIOR - AIRPLANE - FIRST CLASS CABIN - MOMENTS LATER

The plane is airborne, Todd still has his head against the window, looking out at nothing. Another announcement made that electronic devices are now allowed. Todd turns on his phone again, returning his gaze out the window. There is an elderly lady sitting next to him, she is talking across the aisle to someone else. Todd is still unaware of anything around him. He checks the phone, opens it to the apps and begins looking through the photos in the album on his phone. Most are Martin, a few of landscapes, buildings, etc. He stops on one that is similar to the one that was on Martin's iPad, but it is Martin with the black and white cat, grown. Martin pushes up the shade on the window, it's dark out, only the plane in the next gate is visible. Todd gets a vacant look in his eyes.

                              FLASHBACK

EXTERIOR - TODD AND MARTINS HOUSE - YEARS EARLIER - DAYTIME

Todd is out in the yard, raking up small piles of yard debris, when a small pick up truck pulls up, Martin's Vespa scooter in the back. Todd does not recognize the driver of the pick up truck, but Martin gets out of the passenger side, holding a small box, with his messenger bag slung over his shoulder. Todd watches as Martin speaks with the driver a moment, then calls out for Todd.

                    MARTIN
(affectionately) Hey! Mister! Help me get this out of the bed, would ya?

Todd walks over to the truck, as Martin sets the small box on the ground.

                    MARTIN
              Careful of this....

                     TODD
            (to the driver) Hey, I'm Todd.

MARTIN
Todd, this is .....

RANDY
Randy.

MARTIN
...Randy. Randy, this is my Todd. (to Todd) Randy was kind enough to help me get this home.

Todd and Randy move to the bed of the truck and lift down the scooter.

MARTIN
Hey, Randy, thanks again. A million. Sure you don't need something to drink?

Randy holds up his bottle of soda.

RANDY
No, got it. No sweat. You boys have a great day. You're a hero there, man.

Randy drives off. Todd looks at Martin puzzled.

TODD
What happened to your scooter? Who is "Randy?"

MARTIN
Oh, he's a life saver. I met him in the parking lot of the Post Office. Scooter's fine.

Martin steps back over to the small box and opens it. Inside is a very small young black and white kitten.

TODD
Martin,... NO! (only half serious)

MARTIN
Hey, I saved this guys LIFE! You'd never believe it. I was at the intersection of New Bern and Person and some dude in a beater just THREW this little guy into the road! OUT HIS WINDOW!!

The little kitten seems none the worse for wear. Martin nuzzles it gently.

MARTIN
I ran into the street, nearly got hit twice myself! Some lady was screaming her fool head off. But I saved him!

Martin holds the small kitten high up, arms length.

MARTIN
I didn't want to ride the scooter but before I could call you, this guy Randy, he saw the whole thing, he offered to just give me a lift, he had the truck, thank God.

Martin hands the kitten to Todd, who takes it reluctantly. But he is won over and scratches his head.

					TODD
Well, damn. I guess we're cat lovers now. You're going to feed him, brush him and take him for walks, help him with his homework?

					MARTIN
Silly. I promise. Our mom had allergies and we could only have a pet if we kept the house CLEAN! Of course, we only ever had the one dog. Well, and a hamster.

					TODD
What's this guys name? Butch? Fido? Killer?

					MARTIN
					Oweo.

					TODD
					ummm.. What?

					MARTIN
Oweo. You know, like Oreo. Black and white. But no trademark issue.

Todd laughs. He holds the kitten up too for a moment.

					TODD
					Oweo. Perfect.

DISSOLVE

INTERIOR - TODD AND MARTINS HOME - KITCHEN - A FEW YEARS LATER - EVENING

Martin is at the sink, he has finished washing two small bowls, he dries them. Turns to the small table, it has some newspaper on it. He begins wrapping the bowls in the paper silently. Todd enters from the living room.

                    TODD
                (softly) You ok?

                   MARTIN
               Oh yeah, its fine.

                    TODD
This is the shitty part of having pets, man. Chances are you will outlive them.

                   MARTIN
I know. He was a tough guy. Feline leukemia. Who knew?

                    TODD
Don't beat yourself up, he was sliding fast.

Martin picks up a small tin, covered with paw prints. It says OWEO on a small decal from a cheap computer printer.

MARTIN
Ugh. So tacky.

TODD
I don't know protocol. You wanna get a nicer... vessel? Urn? what?

MARTIN
Oh, no! I don't want to keep his ashes, do you?

TODD
I don't know, aren't we supposed to?

MARTIN
Im sure a lot of people do, but no thanks. What? Im gonna put it on a shelf? In a drawer? I don't want my memories tied to some cheap coffee can knock off or even an antique jewelry box.

TODD
Didn't you say you believe animals had souls? How do you want to .... I don't know..."honor" him? Whatever you want, baby.

Martin has finished wrapping the bowls. He secures them together with some masking tape. He picks up the tin again.

MARTIN
I don't know. I'll donate the bowls to a shelter I guess. I wouldn't use them again. No point in saving them. And let's just spread his ashes at the ocean, at the beach.

TODD
Why the ocean? He never left the back yard.

MARTIN
I can't explain it. Whatever it was that "made him up" isn't gone. It's just back to another form of some kind. You know, the law of energy. Never destroyed, just changes. Einstein? Newton? Hawking? Whatever.

Martin sits down beside Todd. Todd reaches over and just rubs Martins forearm in a gentle caress.

MARTIN
I'd like to think that after I die, if you have to decide, that you will cremate me too. Take me to the lake in Chicago, or the beach in Florida. Whatever remains of my physical body, just return it to the water, to the air. It won't be "me" anyway. The part of me that you keep is not physical anyway. And I hate the idea of visiting a cemetery for anyone. It's not like we picnic in graveyards or created memories there. All those poor souls. Doomed to wait in a cemetery for visitors. Visitors. who will someday just stop coming.

                    TODD
Well, until they get their own place there, I guess.

                    MARTIN
It all seems so vain. So pointless. Scatter my ashes someplace you love. Someplace you'd like to think of me. That's where I want my memories to be. What would you want done?

                    TODD
Well, we can do whatever you like with Oweo, but can we not talk about either one of us and the afterlife just yet?

                    MARTIN
Fine by me. If you want something particular though, write it out. You're the thorough one anyway.

                                        FLASHBACK ENDS

INTERIOR - AIRPLANE - FIRST CLASS CABIN

Todd closes out of the phone and rests his head back against the window.

                    TODD
(barely a whisper) Just don't use him to punish me. Just let me get there.

                                        CUT TO

INTERIOR - HOSPITAL - ROOM
CONTINOUS

Sandie is scrolling through the photos on Martin's iPad. There are so many of Todd, Martin and Todd, a few of her own children with her. There are a few of public art (continued) pieces, some with Martin, dressed in a suit, shaking hands with some officials as ribbons are cut or sculptures unveiled.

                    SANDIE
I promise Marty. I will make cookies for you guys every week.

At that moment, Martin's body starts to shake, the beeping of the monitors changes to an urgent tone, Sandie bolts upright out of the chair, just as she makes a decision to turn towards the door, two medical staff rush in, one pushes a button beside the bed, another comes to the door, then turns and dashes out. Martin's body goes still.

                    SANDIE
What? What? What is happening?!

Several hospital staff appear, two of them with extra equipment to transport Martin back to the OR, a doctor is checking Martin for vitals and opening his eyes, looking.

                    DOCTOR
            He's crashing, get the cart!

Two staff bring in a defibrillator as the doctor pulls away the sheer gown that was draped over Martin, pulling away the blanket that had been up to his knees. Sandie is horrified.

                    SANDIE
            No, Marty, no! Wait!

                    DOCTOR
            Got him, lets go!

The medical team continue to work feverishly, the doctor barking orders. They begin wheeling him out, one nurse dragging the IV while another has intubated and is forcing air into Martin's lungs. They disappear out of the room in a chaos, leaving Sandie, standing alone.

                                        CUT TO

INTERIOR - AIRPLANE - FIRST CLASS CABIN
CONTINUOUS

Flight crew are announcing the arrival time of Todd's flight. They are on schedule, to land shortly. They begin coming through the cabins, taking some of the cups and napkins. In first class, things are a little more subdued.

An attendant approaches Todd.

> FLIGHT ATTENDANT
> Sir, we are going to land shortly. Can I get you anything at all. before we ready for arrival?

> TODD
> You know what? Yes, can I please get a vodka. Just one. And a cup of ice.

> FLIGHT ATTENDANT
> Certainly, I don't want to rush you, I'll check with you last thing before landing.

Flight attendant comes right back with a mini of vodka and a small cup of ice. Todd holds up his hand in a gesture signifying her to wait just a moment. He opens the vodka, pours it over the ice, then drinks it in just a few swallows, hands it all back to the flight attendant.

> TODD
> (slight choke) Thank you.

The flight attendant looks at Todd, puzzled.

> FLIGHT ATTENDANT
> Are you certain you wouldn't care for anything else?

				TODD
			That's it, thanks.

Todd turns his head back to the window. The flight attendant walks off.

							FLASHBACK

INTERIOR - TODD AND MARTINS HOME - LIVING ROOM - A YEAR PRIOR - EVENING

Todd, Martin, Sandie and a lesbian couple, Steph and Brenda, are watching a television newscast as a reporter is relaying a story about another states vote to allow marriage equality. All but Sandie send up a whoop.

				BRENDA
	Heck yeah! Steph, we have another option to plan a fancy shin-dig!

				STEPH
	We just need one closer to home. I don't want to deal with travel plans for two families, most of whom haven't been out of the south since the northern aggression.

				TODD
		OK, this calls for a shot!

                                MARTIN
           (surprised) You? You're going to have a shot? Are you
                                  sure?

                                 TODD
              Just one. We don't have champagne. Who's with me?
                             Steph? Brenda?

Hands are raised except for Sandie's. Todd notices.

                                 TODD
              Sandie, how about you help me get them ready?

Martin looks at Sandie, no words exchanged. Sandie doesn't look at Martin.

                                SANDIE
                                Ooooooo k

Sandie gets up and heads into the kitchen behind Todd.

                                                              CUT TO

INTERIOR - TODD AND MARTINS HOME - KITCHEN CONTINUOUS

Todd heads over to a cabinet, getting a few small jelly jars, one for each. He reaches into a cabinet and pulls out a premium tequila. Sandie fidgets just a bit.

SANDIE
um... You really need my help?

TODD
Well... what are your thoughts?

SANDIE
About tequila? Whatever. I didn't think you drank.

TODD
I try not to. I know that Martin used to drink a lot. He never called himself an alcoholic, really, but he said he went through recovery. I've seen him drink on maybe four occasions since I've known him. But no, I meant what do you think about marriage being legal between two guys?

SANDIE
Or women.

TODD
Yeah, (laughs) or two women. I'd love to go to Steph and Brenda's wedding, if they have one. Those chicks can throw a mean barbecue.

SANDIE
Look, I know you and Marty have a real relationship. But marriage, it's kind of.... I don't know.... why would two guys feel the need to get married?

Todd stops pouring the tequila, he looks at Sandie for a long moment, finishes the last pour, recaps the bottle.

                    TODD
        Love, Sandie. Love. (pause) That's why.

                    SANDIE
Well, I don't know, why cant you just have a civil union or something. You're not even religious. Why would YOU think about getting "married?" ARE you?

                    TODD
To be honest, I don't really have a strong desire to, but Martin mentions it from time to time. We say "my husband." He totally loves the idea that it's a declaration. Not just celebrating a relationship, but kind of asking friends and family to support you, help keep two people together, no matter what. Like, it takes a village to raise a marriage.

                    SANDIE
            Yeah, that sounds like him.

Todd laughs a bit. He reaches into the fridge, gets two limes, gets a knife, grabs a salt pig from the stove. He pulls an old wooden tray from the top of the refrigerator. He gets a cutting board and starts cutting the limes into slices.

                    TODD
I'd do it for him. Someday. Maybe. I don't know. But I do
know that I love him, Sandie. He once said "sharing
coffee rings are just as important as sharing wedding
rings" but he loved the idea of sharing a commitment
        with all those who love us and who we love.

Todd looks directly at Sandie, almost challenging her to
meet his gaze. She does.

                    SANDIE
  I don't doubt that. But maybe it's different. It has a
                    different....

                    TODD
                    Purpose?

                    SANDIE
Well, maybe. I mean. I assume from things you've said
that you didn't grow up religious, but what if its against
God's plan? To Marty, that still might matter. He wont
              talk to me about it though.

                    TODD
                    I see.

Todd finishes the cutting, arranges all the cups on a
small tray with the limes and the salt. He returns to the
cabinet and gets two more jelly jars. He pours a small
shot in each.

TODD
Think about this. You love Martin.

SANDIE
Yes, of course.

TODD
Your parents, you loved them. Ed, your kids. Even some of your friends. You love them too, right?

SANDIE
(nodding slightly) Yes.

TODD
Well, I assume you have a different idea of what that means for each one of them, for Martin, for Ed, kids, all of them. You LOVE them, but the love is... individualized. Its a special love you share with each one. It doesn't diminish the love you feel for any of the others.

Sandie is quiet. Todd hands her one of the extra shots of tequila with a lime. He holds up his glass, waiting for her to clink.

TODD
If your God exists and I've not EVER said that I don't believe that He does, but IF He does, certainly His idea and experience of love for all of His children is even deeper and more all encompassing than what we, frail,

imperfect humans can muster. You wouldn't want to hedge your bets AGAINST that would you?

Sandie doesn't say anything. Todd raises his small glass just a bit higher, encouraging Sandie to salute the shot with him.

            TODD
Love is love, Sandie. You should be grateful that there is a lot more of it than you realized before.

Sandie slowly clinks her small glass to Todd's, her facial expression doesn't change. They down the shots and bite the limes.

Todd smiles.

            MARTIN
(from the other room) WHERES THE HOOCH???

                              FLASHBACK ENDS

INTERIOR - AIRPLANE - FIRST CLASS CABIN

The announcement is made as the plane is taxiing into the gate on arrival. Passengers are not getting up yet, but they are going through the normal arranging of their items that were stored under seats, etc. Todd switches his phone back to cellular mode. He dials Sandie's number. It doesn't go through, beeps as the call is dropped. Todd grimaces and tries again. The plane has reached the gate and the passengers are up and gathering bags from the overhead. Todd stands, excuses himself to the elderly lady beside him, edges around her, pulls his carry-on from the compartment. He stands in the aisle, he starts to get a worried look on his face as he tries calling again. The call drops. The cabin door is opened and he makes a mad dash past the flight crew as they thank the passengers.

                                                        CUT TO

INTERIOR - RDU AIRPORT -
A FEW MOMENTS LATER

Todd walks quickly, not quite a run, into the airport. There are still plenty of folks around, coming and going. He dashes past the exit, opposite the line of passengers going through airport security.

EXTERIOR - RDU AIRPORT -
CONTINUOUS

He looks about wildly, getting his bearings, then dodges and weaves past people, he hurries past the baggage claim and out into the passenger pick up, sees a cab assist, yells out.

                    TODD
    Hey! Hey buddy! Can you get me a cab? Right away!

The cab assist waves at a cab in their wait area, one jumps to life and glides up beside Todd. Todd throws a five dollar bill at the cab assist, jumping into the cab.

INTERIOR - CAB - CONTINUOUS

                    TODD
I need to get to Raleigh Memorial, as quickly as you can. Take me to the Emergency entrance.

The cab driver doesn't say anything, he has an earpiece and quietly speaks into it, obviously on the phone with someone else. The cab lurches into the lane exiting the airport area.

EXTERIOR - AIRPORT - EXIT LANES

The cab accelerates into exiting traffic.

INTERIOR - CAB - CONTINUOUS

Todd takes a deep breath, trying to calm himself. He stretches out his arms, exhales. He tries dialing the iPad, the call is not answered.

                    TODD
            Dammit, c'mon Sandie,

Todd dials Sandie again, this time it goes to voice mail. Todd leaves a message.

                    TODD
Hey, it's me. Not sure if you are talking to the doctors or what. I'm here. I'm freaking out, but I'm on my way in a cab, left my car at the airport so I won't have to deal with hospital parking, so maybe twenty minutes. When you get this, just call me.

Todd sends a text to Sandie. "spotty reception maybe, I'm in a cab on way. Call ASAP." He sends message. He dials 411 information.

                    TODD
         Raleigh Memorial, admitting?

He holds, presses a single button on the phone, puts the phone back to his ear.

                    TODD
Yes, I'm looking for a patient, Martin Raymond. (pause) No, I'm aware of that, can you tell me if he has been admitted? (pause) Well then can you page his sister for me? She's there with him. (pause) NO, she is not a patient, (pause) well, can you transfer me to whatever station may know? (pause) OK, OK, (pause) yes, I understand. (pause) Thanks anyway....

Todd ends the call.

EXTERIOR - CAB PULLS ONTO RALEIGH HIGHWAY

Martin looks out the window, lights reflected across his face. The cab is driving through medium traffic, cityscape evident.

                              FLASHBACK

MONTAGE: TODD AND MARTIN, VARYING ACTIVITIES OF A NORMAL COUPLE, WASHING A CAR, MARTIN MAKING A COLLAGE, DRINKING COFFEE, ARGUING, SITTING TOGETHER IN A THEATER,

EXTERIOR - MOVIE THEATRE - TEN YEARS PRIOR - NIGHT

Todd is waiting for Martin outside of a small, art house theater. "The Color Purple" is being billed with a "Movies We Love" banner. Martin comes up, a bit breathless. Todd gets a big smile.

                    TODD
     Hey, there you are. Wow, you're a punctual guy too.
                  Right on.

Todd offers his hand to shake just as Martin was leaning in for a chaste hug, they end in an awkward half hug.

MARTIN

Sorry, I don't know what "first date rules" dictate. Just thought I'd hug you now in case you're a bad date.

TODD

(laughs nervously) All good. It takes me a while to be a social hugger.

MARTIN

No judgment. I don't like to share straws or toothbrushes. (he winks) Thanks for agreeing to this one. I know it's old, but it's only here the one night and I really really wanted to catch it.

TODD

Just so I don't put my foot in it, what are the rules for buying tickets and snacks? (he holds up the tickets) I already bought the tickets.

MARTIN

Well, halvesies. Since you bought the tickets, I will buy the snacks. Although, unless you think I'm made of money, no extra large tubs of popcorn.

Todd laughs. They head into the theater.

INTERIOR - MOVIE THEATER - ABOUT TWO HOURS LATER

Todd looks over at Martin, who has tears in his eyes.

Todd seems transfixed by the film. We hear the music swell in the background.

CUT TO

EXTERIOR - MOVIE THEATRE - TWENTY MINUTES LATER

Todd and Martin have exited the theater. They are standing outside the theater as people are coming and going.

TODD
You wanna walk a bit?

MARTIN
Sure.

They head off down the sidewalk. There are a few people milling about, they walk slowly, passing a restaurant or two. They are quiet for a moment.

TODD
It was a pretty emotional film. I saw it years ago obviously, but it seems even better now. I didn't realize you hadn't seen it before. I saw you got choked up quite a bit.

MARTIN
Oh, I've seen it dozens of times. Maybe a hundred.

Todd looks at Martin, slightly puzzled.

                    TODD
        A hundred times? And it still makes you cry?

                    MARTIN
        I own it on DVD still. Yeah, it gets to me every time. (he looks at Todd) But thanks. I'm glad this was a first date.

Todd seems moved at Martin's reaction. They share a half smile with each other. Martin looks down and Todd's smile gets bigger.

They continue walking.

                                        FLASHBACK ENDS

EXTERIOR - HOSPITAL - EMERGENCY ENTRANCE - MOMENTS LATER

The cab pulls up and Todd pays the driver, he gets out pulling his bag behind him. He runs into the hospital and goes to the security desk.

                                        CUT TO

INTERIOR - HOSPITAL - ER ADMITTING CONTINUOUS

Todd is stopped by security, who want to check his bags, he hands his ID to the admitting.

TODD
Can you tell me where Martin Raymond is? Or page his sister, Sandie Allen. He was brought in this afternoon, an accident?

ADMITTING
Please sir, just a moment, let me scan your ID..... here (hands Todd a print out visitors badge, basically a label maker, but it has his ID photo and name on it) Let me see, ... um.... I cannot tell you anything here, but if you can go to the second hallway, on your right. There is a desk about halfway down the hallway, on your right. Thats a waiting area and you can check there.

The admitting clerk looks over at the security.

ADMITTING
(to security, quietly) Can you just put those in the holding area, Mr... (she checks the print out again, looks at Todd) Mr. Gordon, you can come back for your things after you speak with the doctor. I will page him and let him know to meet you there.

TODD
Second hallway, right, down that hallway, halfway

                    ADMITTING
        halfway, yes sir. Dr. Daniels, I believe will meet you
                            there.

                            TODD
        Thank you, (turns to security) You can keep this here?
                    (indicates the suitcase)

                          SECURITY
                Yes sir, I'll put your name on it.

                            TODD
                      Thanks, yeah, thanks.

Todd walks quickly down the hall indicated, turns right down second adjoining hallway, as his focus clears, he sees Sandie.

                                                WIDE SHOT

Sandie is standing with her husband Ed, who is holding her, and her two children are crying and hugging their parents around their legs. Todd stops. Ed notices and whispers something to Sandie. She looks up to see Todd. She is obviously bereft.

Todd doesn't move, he just looks at her. She slowly shakes her head. Todd drops his messenger bag, collapses onto one knee, looks as if he is going to pass out.

Sandie leaves her husband, who gathers the kids to him. Sandie wraps her arms tightly around herself. Todd has stood up, but not come forward. Sandie reaches him. Sandie just stands in front of him. She is shaking but still has not unwrapped her arms from herself. Todd chokes out a sob.

We see a doctor approach from a hallway, he sees Sandie and begins to head in that direction. Ed stops him.

CLOSE UP: DR DANIELS AND ED

ED
Dr. Daniels, wait. (pause, then quietly) Just a moment.

DR DANIELS
Who is that? Is he your family as well?

ED
That's Mr. Gordon,

EVIE
(crying) That's Uncle Todd.

ED
My brother-in-law. We're HIS family.

WIDE: HOSPITAL HALLWAY

The doctor stays beside Ed. Sandie is in front of Todd, who has not spoken. Sandie finally unfolds her arms, she is afraid to touch Todd. Todd finally looks at her, focusing. He breaks down and she hugs him closely.

DISSOLVE

INTERIOR - TODD AND MARTINS HOME - LIVING ROOM
PRESENT DAY

REPLAY OF SCENE 12

Todd moves to a box that is on a table and pulls out an urn. We see that it is a simple funerary urn that would hold ashes of cremains and a label on the box reads "Martin Raymond; Gilbert Funeral Home."

TODD

Yeah, it was nice. That's what you say right? That's what everyone says. "It was nice." (Pause) More for them, than for me. (Pause) He wanted to be taken to the beach. I owe that to him. (voice cracks) I'm leaving him there.

TODD (VO)

No, I couldn't leave you unless I loved you. I'd want you with me always. Even like this..

He sets the urn down with his back to the camera.

CAMERA VIEW BEGINS TO WIDEN OUT SLOWLY.

Todd returns to phone conversation as scene begins to WHITE OUT.

                  TODD

I will call you when I land. I can finish things here any time. (Pause) I just can't believe I'm doing this.

                            WIDE SHOT

Todd continues to talk on the phone, we do not hear what is being said from other end. We see the framed mementos.

We hear Martin's voice in Todd's head, as he recalls a conversation.

                  MARTIN (VO)

(quietly) Who knows when we will smell something like this again, but when we do, just know one thing....

                  TODD (VO)
                  Whats that?

                  MARTIN (VO)
That I love you Todd. Really, really.

                  TODD (VO)
                  Oh wow.

                    MARTIN (VO)
    Breathe that in. I love you. You don't have to say
    anything. But someday, if you smell this again. You
                    WILL remember.

Voice over memory ends.

                         TODD
    Yeah, thanks hon. I love you too. (pause) I promise.
    Hey, the orange trees... how long before they bloom?
         (pause) OK, yes, see you soon. (pause) Bye.

Todd ends the call. He sits down next to the bag he has packed to travel, still holding the urn. He looks up, not focusing on anything in particular.

                         TODD
              Martin, I love you. Really really.

                                                    CUT TO

EXTERIOR - TODD AND MARTINS HOUSE

                                                   FADE OUT

                           END

About the Author

Brian Todd Barnette was born in Melbourne, Florida. He spent most of his "growing up years" between Florida and North Carolina attending both UNC Wilmington, and UCF-Orlando. He graduated with a B.A. in Psychology.

Brian enjoys self directed study in motivation and self improvement, inter- personal dynamics, and meta-physics. He has led many discussion groups and has given spiritual consultations to those seeking a better personal understanding of themselves. His interests are in development, enlightenment, and personal growth.

Bits and Peaces Productions™ is a media company, created by Brian Todd Barnette.

Information can be found at
www.BITSandPEACESproductions.com

BITS AND PEACES
PRODUCTIONS™

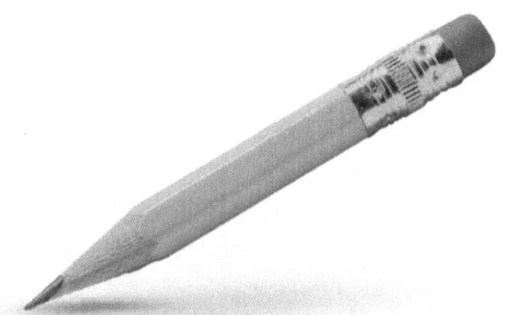

More to come...

www.ingramcontent.com/pod-product-compliance
Lightning Source LLC
Chambersburg PA
CBHW031417290426
44110CB00011B/413